T-B
ROBES-   McGowen, Tom
PIERRE   Robespierre and the
                French Revolution in

ROBESPIERRE and the FRENCH REVOLUTION
in World History

Tom McGowen

Enslow Publishers, Inc.

40 Industrial Road   PO Box 38
Box 398   Aldershot
Berkeley Heights, NJ 07922   Hants GU12 6BP
USA   UK

http://www.enslow.com

T-B
ROBESPIERRE

Library of Congress Cataloging-in-Publication Data

McGowen, Tom.
 Robespierre and the French Revolution in world history / Tom
McGowen.
   p. cm. — (In world history)
  Includes bibliographical references and index.
  Summary: Traces the history of the French Revolution from the
storming of the Bastille through the rise of Napoleon, highlighting the
influence of revolutionary leader, Maximilien Robespierre, from his early
life through his involvement in the Reign of Terror.
  ISBN 0-7660-1397-9
  1. Robespierre, Maximilien, 1758–1794 Juvenile literature. 2. France—
History—Revolution, 1789–1799 Juvenile literature. 3. Revolutionaries—
France—Biography Juvenile literature. 4. France—History—Reign of
terror, 1793–1794 Juvenile literature. [1. Robespierre, Maximilien,
1758–1794. 2. Revolutionaries. 3. France—History—Revolution,
1789–1799. 4. France—History—Reign of terror, 1793–1794.] I. Title.
II. Series.
DC146.R6M37 2000
944.04'092—dc21
[B]
                 99-41656
                 CIP

Printed in the United States of America

10 9 8 7 6 5 4 3 2

Illustration Credits: Corel Corporation, p. 117; Enslow Publishers, Inc.,
pp. 11, 64, 72, 90; John Grafton, *The American Revolution: A Picture
Sourcebook* (New York: Dover Publications, Inc., 1975), p. 30; Library of
Congress, pp. 15, 21, 23, 33, 34, 40, 44, 53, 76, 78, 86, 94, 97, 101, 108, 113,
115; National Library, Paris, France, p. 7.

Cover Illustration: Background Map—© Digital Vision Ltd.; Portrait of
Robespierre—Robespierre by French School (18th century) Musee
Carnavalet, Paris, France/Bridgeman Art Library.

Contents

Chapter 1

A Celebration of Death

A special event was about to take place in the center of a city. The center was a broad, square, open area, with buildings around it on all sides. It was the place where special events and celebrations were often held, and such an event was going to be held on this day. The square was packed with thousands of people jostling and bumping one another, talking excitedly, and gesturing and waving their arms.

At the center of the square was a high wooden platform with steps leading up to it. On the platform was a machine for killing people. This machine, called a guillotine, was made up of two tall wooden posts with a heavy blade suspended high between them. A thick cord held the blade in place. The victim was placed facedown with his or her head between the posts. When the cord was cut, the blade was released to come sliding swiftly down with enough force to slice through the victim's neck.

On this day, on the platform beside the guillotine were several men. These were the executioners—the men who would use the guillotine to cut off the heads of those who had been sentenced to die on this day. The crowd was gathered in the square to watch the execution.

All around the square platform were arranged several rows of chairs and benches. Seated on these were women of all ages. They were in the best place to see everything that would happen up on the platform. Most of the women had balls of yarn in their laps and knitting needles in their hands and were industriously knitting. They talked and laughed as they worked.

The sudden roar of a cheer erupted from the crowd. At one end of the square, a vehicle was emerging from between two buildings. It was a two-wheeled wooden cart, painted red, drawn by a pair of plodding horses. Standing in the cart, behind the driver, were several people, both men and women. Their hands were tied behind their backs.

The crowd parted for the cart, and the horses clip-clopped their way toward the center of the square. The driver brought them to a halt beside the platform. Two of the executioners came down and roughly helped one of the prisoners, a man, out of the cart. Quickly, one of the executioners cut the man's hair short, so it would not get in the way of the guillotine's blade. Then, they led him up the steps, onto the platform.

An artist drew this image of a guillotine, which became the main method of execution during the French Revolution.

The man was pushed down to lie flat on a wooden plank and was strapped into place so he could not move. The plank was shoved forward so that the man's head went into a wooden brace that positioned his neck directly beneath the blade. His head stuck out over a basket that sat on the platform.

One of the executioners cut the cord. The blade hurtled down.

Blood sprayed out over the women in the front row, falling on the objects they were knitting. The women laughed with glee. They were knitting stockings for soldiers who were fighting for the country in foreign lands, and they believed the spots of blood would make the men fight harder.

An executioner reached down into the basket. He lifted up the severed head, blood still dripping from the neck, and held it up for the crowd to see. There was a roar of approval from the people who had watched the execution. They cheered and applauded.

What could cause such a horrible spectacle as this? What could cause ordinary people to turn into savages, rejoicing at the sight of the bloody death of other people?

What caused it was an event that took place more than two hundred years ago in the nation of France. That event is known as the French Revolution. It became a bloody and terrible spectacle. But it began very quietly, in the year 1789.

Chapter 2

A Troubled Nation

As the year 1789 began, the kingdom of France was one of the foremost nations of the world. It had a powerful army and navy, with which it had helped the American colonies win their war for independence from Great Britain. It had colonies and possessions in various parts of the world. It was a leader in science and art and was generally regarded as a steady, intelligent, highly civilized country.

But it was a nation based on feudalism, the system of lords and subjects, as it had been since medieval times. The lords—the king, the nobles, and the high officials of the Catholic Church—had total power over the subjects, the common people. There was no freedom of speech, no freedom of religion, no freedom of the press, and very few freedoms of any other kind.

The Three Estates

The people of France were divided into three classes, or estates. The First Estate was the clergy, or religious workers, making up about one percent of the total population. The French clergy was almost entirely made up of priests and nuns of the Roman Catholic Church. By law, this was the official religion of France. Protestants and Jews were not permitted to worship openly, and there were no other religions in the country.

The Second Estate was the nobility, people who had titles before their name—duke and duchess, count and countess, marquis and marquess. The nobility was composed of some thirty thousand families, about two hundred thousand people. Supposedly, they were descended from warriors who had helped the first king conquer France in ancient times, or from persons who had helped other kings in some way and had been rewarded with wealth, land, and privileges. So, nobles owned much of the land of France. Noblemen commanded the regiments and armies and fleets of the French Army and Navy and were the king's counselors and government officials. They also held most of the positions of highest authority in the Church, because they were appointed to such positions by the king. However, not all nobles were wealthy. Some owned nothing more than a small farm and did much of their own farmwork.

The Third Estate was the commoners, some 26 million strong. There were basically two groups of

FLANDERS
ARTOIS
LILLE
• Douai
Arras •
ROUEN   AMIENS
Rouen •   SOISSONS
NORMANDY   Metz •
CAEN   LORRAINE   ALSACE
• Paris   CHÂLONS   Nancy •
ALENÇON   Versailles •
PARIS   Colmar •
RENNES
• Rennes   ORLEANS   FRANCHE
BRITTANY   Dijon •   COMTÉ
TOURS   Besançon
DIJON /
POITIERS   BOURGES   BURGUNDY
POITOU   MOULINS
DOMBES
LA ROCHELLE   LIMOGES   LYONS
RIOM   Grenoble •
AUVERGNE   GRENOBLE
BORDEAUX   DAUPHINÉ
Bordeaux •
GUYENNE   AIX
MONTAUBAN
AUCH   PROVENCE
BAYONNE   • Toulouse   LANGUEDOC   Aix •
• Pau   MONTPELLIER
• Perpignon
Pre-revolutionary France
PERPIGNAN

Before the revolution, France was divided into many sections, with local governments.

commoners. One group, known in France as the *bourgeoisie*, was what might be called the middle class in America. They were owners of large farms or large or small businesses, shop owners, doctors, lawyers, and judges. These people were generally prosperous, and some were as wealthy as nobles. The other group was the laborers. Many of these were factory workers, dock workers, wagon drivers, grave diggers, or servants who worked for nobles. But most—about 21 million—were peasants, farmers who owned only tiny farms or who lived and worked on farms belonging to nobles or to the Church. Many laborers, especially the peasants, were desperately, agonizingly poor. An Englishman who had traveled through France wrote of seeing many peasants who looked more like skinny scarecrows than human beings. Another English traveler told of ragged, hungry-looking children who made his heart ache.

Poverty, Taxation, and Injustice

But poor or not, nearly all commoners were subject to a great many taxes, payments, and obligations. They had to pay a yearly flat-rate tax (the same amount for everyone) to the government, as well as a kind of income tax consisting of an amount equal to one twentieth of their income. They also had to pay a tithe, equal to the value of one tenth of their income and all their belongings, to the Church. They paid taxes on all the salt, wine, tobacco, soap, leather, and ironware they bought. If they happened to live on land that

Source Document

. . . The abuses attending the levy of taxes were heavy and universal. . . . [W]hat must have been the state of the poor people paying heavy taxes, from which the nobility and clergy were exempted? A cruel aggravation of their misery, to see those who could best afford to pay, exempted because able! . . . The *corvees* [a tax in kind; it was paid through labor service rather than in money], or police of the roads, were annually the ruin of many hundreds of farmers. . . .[1]

British writer Arthur Young described the poverty and corruption he witnessed while traveling in France during the years just before the start of the French Revolution.

belonged to the Church, they paid a tax on that. If they lived on a noble's land, they paid him rent.

Living on a noble's land also meant many additional costs and restrictions. In order to grind any grain they raised into flour, or to press grapes into juice for wine, peasants had to pay a nobleman for the use of his flour mill or winepress. In many places, if there were a bridge crossing a stream on the noble's land, the peasants had to pay a fee for using the bridge. They were responsible for the upkeep and maintenance of all the roads on the land, at their own expense, and this often took them away from their farms—where their efforts were needed to plant or harvest crops that meant their livelihood—for weeks at a time. Worst of all, they were forbidden to hunt or trap any animals on the land. This not only kept them from a valuable food supply, but also meant a loss of some of their crops, because animals and birds ate many of the seeds peasants planted, and then ate much of the plants that grew from the seeds that were left. But a peasant caught trying to prevent this by killing an animal or bird could be shot and killed by the noble's gamekeepers.

Most of the lower ranks of the clergy—parish priests, monsigneurs, and abbots—had come from commoner families and thought of themselves as equal with commoners. But to most nobles, the commoners were far beneath them. Their contemptuous term for commoners was *canaille*, meaning "vulgar," or low and crude.

Resentment and a Wish for New Ways

The nobles and the high officials of the Church were completely free from having to pay most taxes. Thus, the commoners were literally paying the living expenses of the nobles and high Church officials. While a commoner might have to struggle to make enough to feed, dress, and house his family, many nobles were spending millions for nothing more than lavish parties and entertainments. And so, there was bitter resentment among most members of the Third Estate toward the nobles.

There was resentment even among the wealthier people of the Third Estate, the bourgeoisie, especially those who had created large, profitable businesses and industries. Despite their valuable contributions to the economy of France, they were given no more rights than the poorest peasant. They could not dream of ever becoming high-ranking military or naval commanders, officials of the Church, or counselors of the king. Such things were forbidden to them. Like the peasants, they were just *canaille*.

Adding to all this resentment was a flood of new ideas sweeping through France among the educated members of the Third Estate, as well as some nobles and priests. These ideas, known collectively as the

This drawing pokes fun at the overly luxurious lifestyle of the nobles, which the peasants believed was responsible for their own oppression and poverty.

Enlightenment—which meant an opening up of the mind—had been growing for years. Since the 1600s, philosophers throughout Europe, such as the Frenchmen Voltaire and Montesquieu, and the Swiss Jean-Jacques Rousseau, had been writing that the governments and ways of life of nations should be based on logical thinking and science, rather than on old traditions and customs. For these men, such things as kings and nobles and established religions simply were not logical. They argued that all people should be equal and that governments should be based on the needs of all the people, rather than just a privileged few. Seeing this idea as the way to a better life, many members of the bourgeoisie believed France should have a new kind of government. They also wanted more rights for the Third Estate and less for the king, nobles, and Church. Many of them wanted a constitution for France, like the constitution of Great Britain, which provided equal power for king, nobles, and commoners. A few wanted a constitution like that of the United States, with no king, no nobles, and a government controlled by the people. Of course, the king, most of the nobles, and Church officials of France were bitterly opposed to such ideas.

Hunger, Desperation, Violence, and Hope

In addition to the simmering resentment over inequality, there was also concern throughout the Third Estate over the growing difficulty of making a living. France had been involved in a number of wars during the last fifty years. This had cost enormous amounts of money. As a result, the French treasury was nearly empty, and the government had to cut back on many of the things it regularly bought. This hurt business and caused many people to lose their jobs. To make things worse, there had been bad harvests throughout the country, so there was a shortage of grain. Bread, the main food of the poor—for some, their only food—was becoming scarce. It had nearly doubled in price. For years, a family-size four-pound loaf of bread had cost eight sous—around two dollars. Now the price was up to three and even four dollars a loaf. Thus, a farmworker who made only five sous a day, about $1.25, could buy a loaf of bread only every three days. Trying to live for three days on one day's worth of food literally meant starvation for him and his family. Many people could not survive, and hordes of beggars—men, women, and children—began to appear.

Some people became desperate. They began to disobey laws and turn to violence. Throughout the countryside, French peasants banded together. Ignoring the laws that prohibited them from hunting, they began to hunt and trap rabbits, deer, pheasants, and other creatures that by law "belonged" only to the nobles. In some places, when game wardens working for nobles tried to prevent the hunting and trapping, they were simply murdered.

In many farm areas, bands of desperate and hungry people, mainly women determined to see that their families were fed, began to make raids on barges and wagon trains that were bringing grain into the cities. They took what they felt they needed.

In the cities, too, desperate and starving people became violent. In the city of Marseilles, the town hall was stormed and looted. In Aix en Provence, there was a riot. Soldiers called to stop it fired into the crowd, killing several people. In Paris, a rumor began that the wealthy owner of a large, prosperous wallpaper factory had said that wages for workers were too high. A huge crowd of thousands of angry jobless people marched to the factory, chanting, "Death to the rich, death to the aristocrats!"[2] They poured into the factory and set it on fire; then went on to the owner's nearby house and looted and destroyed that. Soldiers appeared. Here, too, they fired into the crowd. Some six hundred people were killed or wounded.

Thus, as the year 1789 slipped into spring, there was resentment, anger, fear, and violence spreading throughout the French nation. Everyone felt that something had to be done, soon, to make things better. Their one great hope lay in an event that was going to happen in May of that year in a little town called Versailles, where there was a splendid royal palace. There was going to be a great meeting held there. Men representing each of the three estates were going to get together to try to solve France's troubles. And so, as the trees began to sprout buds and the air began to grow warm, the eyes and thoughts of all France were on Versailles.

One of the people who had Versailles uppermost in his mind was a thirty-year-old lawyer living in the northern town of Arras. He had been selected to go to Versailles as one of the representatives of the Third Estate. His name was Maximilien François Marie Isadore de Robespierre.

Rumblings of Revolt

The king of France, Louis XVI, was a chubby, not very good-looking man, who was thirty-five years old as 1789 began. He tended to eat and drink too much and fall asleep during important meetings and events. He was interested in mechanical things, and his hobby was making locks and keys. But what he loved more than anything else was to go hunting. Most people of France believed that Louis was king because God wanted him to be. He was what is known as an absolute monarch, meaning that he had total, absolute power over everyone and everything. However, Louis was not a tyrant. Actually, he did not really much want to be king, but he sincerely tried to do his best. He was well liked by most of the French people.

This was not true of his queen, however. Her name was Marie Antoinette, and she was not a French

The indecisive King Louis XVI was, at first, popular with the French people.

woman. She was an Austrian, the sister of the emperor of the Austrian-Hungarian Empire. She had been reared as a princess with every luxury and had become rather vain and self-centered. She spent enormous amounts of money on clothes, cosmetics, and hairstyles. She also spent a great amount of time and money trying to keep herself amused. She was able to talk the king into doing just about anything she wanted him to do.

The king had two younger brothers: the Comte (Count) d'Artois and the Comte de Provence. He also had two sisters—Clotilde, who was married to the king of Sardinia, and Elizabeth. Louis paid for nearly everything Elizabeth and his brothers did, including gambling debts. He also listened to their advice, which usually was not very good. Marie Antoinette and the Comte d'Artois often teamed up to convince Louis what he ought to do.

Louis was very much concerned about the problems of his nation in 1789, particularly the lack of money. But he was the sort of person who, when confronted with a problem, simply ignored it, apparently hoping it would just go away. He left most decisions to his counselors.

One of his major counselors was the minister of finance, the person who was responsible for seeing that France had enough money. Louis's minister of finance was a Swiss man by the name of Jacques Necker. Necker had been a banker in Switzerland. He understood a great deal about how to raise money and

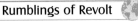

This is an artist's depiction of the royal family. Louis XVI is at right and Marie Antoinette is at left.

invest it to make it grow. However, Switzerland was a republic, with no king or nobles, so Necker was a commoner. The French nobles, including the queen and the king's two brothers, did not like him. He had once published a report that showed how much of the tax money spent in France went to support the nobles, and one of his main ideas for raising money to refill the French treasury was to tax the nobles and the clergy. Of course, the nobles were completely against this. They let it be known that they would refuse to accept such a change in their way of life. However, the Third Estate felt that Necker was on their side and looked on him as a friend.

The Estates-General—A Meeting of the Three Estates

To help solve France's problems, Necker and some of the king's other counselors advised Louis to call a great meeting to which elected representatives of each of the three estates could come to offer their ideas. Such meetings had been called before, by past kings, and were known as Estates-General. So, in the summer of 1788, Louis had ordered the members of the three estates in each region of France to hold elections and select delegates to represent them at the Estates-General, to be held in 1789. He also ordered the members of each estate to draw up lists of grievances, or complaints, about matters affecting them that seemed unfair or unjust.

To most members of the Third Estate, this looked like an answer to their prayers. Not only was the king going to try to solve the problems of food and money, but he was also apparently going to do something about all the injustices they were suffering from taxes and the special privileges of the First and Second Estates. People of every region began to list their protests, and these turned out to be much alike everywhere. They wanted taxes made the same for everyone, with the nobles and clergy paying taxes as commoners did. They wanted freedom of the press, with no more censorship of books, newspapers, or magazines. They wanted greater religious freedom, at least for Protestants. There were many demands for more freedom, for more equality, and for a constitution for France.

In late April, the delegates began to arrive in the town of Versailles. The representatives of the Third Estate consisted of 178 merchants and shopkeepers, 158 judges of low courts, and 214 lawyers. One of these was Maximilien de Robespierre, delegate from the region of Artois, in the far north of France.

Maximilien de Robespierre

Maximilien de Robespierre was born in 1758, the first child of a well-to-do family. His father was a lawyer. By the time Maximilien was six, he had a brother and two sisters, but it was then that his mother died. Soon after, his father abandoned the four children to relatives and left town. From then on, Maximilien was reared by two aunts.

When he was eleven, he won a scholarship to one of the best schools in France, located in Paris. He lived at the school for the next twelve years and was regarded as a brilliant student. After graduating, he became a lawyer and returned to his town of Arras, where he lived with his brother and sisters.

Maximilien was small and slim, with a high, wide forehead; a long, thin nose; and watery, red-rimmed eyes. In Versailles, he dressed very carefully, in a worn black suit, and his hair was always perfectly arranged

25

and powdered, which was then the style. None of the other delegates knew much about him, but in Arras, he was known as a staunch defender of the poor. He had been the lawyer for many poor people, trying to gain justice for them and prevent them from being treated unfairly. As the other delegates got to know him, they learned that Robespierre admired the great philosopher Rousseau tremendously. Like Rousseau, he was a fiercely intense believer in democracy, or government of the people.

Another of the delegates was a forty-year-old man who was well-known to everyone. He was the Comte de Mirabeau, a strange-looking person with a bulky body and huge head and neck. As a child, he had suffered from the disease known as smallpox, which covered a person's body with blisters that generally left scars, and Mirabeau's big face was pitted and pocked with such scars. His great-great-grandfather had been a commoner who was made a noble by a past king, so Mirabeau was technically a nobleman. However, most nobles whose families went back many hundreds of years looked down on such people, and Mirabeau had often been treated with contempt. So although he believed in monarchy, rule by a king, Mirabeau hated the nobility and had come to the Estates-General as a delegate of the Third Estate. He was known as a powerful speaker, who could excite people with his voice and words. He also had a reputation as a wild, partying sort of person.

Insults and Humiliation for the Third Estate

The meeting of the Estates-General was to begin on May 5, 1789. But even before the meeting started, it quickly began to look as if attempts were going to be made to keep the delegates of the Third Estate "in their place." All of them had been instructed to wear only black clothes, the traditional garb of the low class. When they went to meet the king in the great palace of Versailles, they were allowed to enter only through side doors. Instead of meeting with all the delegates at once, the king met first with the delegates of the First Estate and then with the nobles of the Second Estate, in his own private rooms. Then, after making the Third Estate delegates wait a long time, the king met with them in another room. He did not speak to any of them except for one elderly man. Most of them felt slighted.

More slights were to come. The next day, when all the delegates went to church for a special mass, the First and Second Estate delegates all had reserved seats, but the Third Estate delegates were left to find their own places. In the parade of delegates that marched through the streets of Versailles, the men of the Third Estate were put at the front, which actually meant that they were considered of least importance.

The meeting of the Estates-General was held in a large hall of a building that generally was used as a theater where plays were performed. The meeting began with a short speech by the king. He did not mention any of the issues the Third Estate delegates were most concerned about, such as more rights for the commoners and a reduction of taxes. He seemed concerned only with raising money for the French treasury. Then there was a long, dry, droning speech by Necker, finished by one of his secretaries, which was also about raising money. It began to seem to the Third Estate delegates as if no attention at all were going to be paid to the wishes and ideas of the common people.

The next day, the delegates of the three estates were split up into three rooms. The meeting was arranged so that the delegates of each estate, after discussing matters among themselves and coming to an agreement, would cast a single vote representing their decision. Thus, each estate had one vote. What this meant, of course, was that the First and Second Estates would be able to outvote the Third Estate, two to one. Thus, the delegates representing only about 4 percent of France would have more power than the delegates representing 96 percent! The Third Estate would never have a chance to make any of the changes it was hoping for.

The Third Estate Becomes the National Assembly

The Third Estate could not agree to this. Their wish was that the delegates of the three estates should all meet together, and that every delegate of each estate should have one vote. The problems facing the nation could be discussed, debated, and voted on, with the majority vote winning. In other words, they wanted a *democratic* way of voting. That way, the Third Estate delegates, with the help of votes from members of the First and Second Estates who agreed with them, might be able to gain some of the changes they wanted.

There were delegates of the First and Second Estates who were willing to side with the Third Estate. Among the First Estate delegates were many ordinary priests who wanted to help reduce the taxes and restrictions on the desperately poor peasants and who bitterly detested the noble bishops, archbishops, and cardinals, who possessed enormous wealth. There were clear-thinking noblemen who realized that the situation in France had to be changed, or the country would simply come apart. One of these was the Marquis de Lafayette, who had fought on the American side in the American Revolution and was regarded as a hero in both the United States and France. It was Lafayette who first suggested the idea of holding a meeting of the Estates-General.

But the high officials of the Church and the majority of nobles of the Second Estate were well aware that they could lose their power if the method of voting was changed. They utterly refused to accept any change.

Days went by. Nothing happened and nothing was accomplished. Then, both de Robespierre, who was now calling himself Robespierre, and Mirabeau suggested that the clergymen be invited to join with the Third Estate delegates in an effort to make some progress. The invitation was made.

The Marquis de Lafayette, who had served as an officer under George Washington during the American Revolution, became one of the most famous figures in the French Revolution.

This caused a tumult among the delegates of the First Estate. Many priests wanted to join the Third Estate delegates, but the noble archbishops, bishops, and cardinals refused to consider such an idea.

However, the delegates of the Third Estate had come to the Estates-General specifically to present the wishes and demands of the commoners to the king, and that was what they intended to do. For days, they talked matters over among themselves. One of the delegates, a clergyman named Sieyès, pointed out that the Third Estate represented more than 96 percent of the French population, which was basically the entire

Source Document

Art. 70. We demand, for the benefit of commerce, the abolition of all exclusive privileges:

* The removal of customs barriers to the frontiers;
* The most complete freedom in trade;
* The revision and reform of all laws relative to commerce;
* Encouragement for all kinds of manufacture, viz.: premiums, bounties and advances;
* Rewards to artisans and laborers for useful inventions.[1]

The Third Estate, made up of representatives of the common people, drew up this list of demands they hoped to get from the French government in 1789.

French nation. Therefore, the Third Estate delegates could claim that only they actually represented the nation. Another delegate suggested they should give themselves the name of National Assembly, to show this. This was voted on, and the name was accepted by 491 votes. The delegates then started to work on the creation of new laws and decrees for things the commoners wanted.

The Beginning of the Revolution

On June 19, the majority of priest-delegates of the First Estate voted to join the National Assembly. This meant that power was now in the hands of the Third Estate. A cardinal and archbishop of the First Estate and several noblemen of the Second Estate rushed to see the king. Desperately, they urged him to halt the entire meeting of the Estates-General and bring it to an end.

The king did not know what to do. Necker suggested that he agree to many of the things the Third Estate wanted, which would make him tremendously popular with the commoners. But the queen and the king's two brothers argued that Louis could not give in to the commoners. They insisted that he had to show his power and do something to keep the Third Estate delegates in their place.

Thus, on the morning of June 20, when the members of the National Assembly went to begin their meeting, they found the room locked and under guard. They were told that it was being made ready for

This cartoon celebrates the union of the three estates—the nobility, the clergy, and the common people—to make revolutionary changes in the government of France.

a special meeting the king intended to hold and could not be used until then. This not only prevented them from meeting, but also kept the clergymen from officially joining them. They felt sure this was really just the first step in an attempt to break them up and force them to leave Versailles.

They determined to strike back. In a drizzling rain, they all walked through the streets of Versailles until they found a building large enough to hold them, which was an indoor tennis court, and took it over for

Representatives held their own meeting at a tennis court after being barred from the official one. There, they took the so-called Tennis Court Oath.

their meeting. All but one of the delegates swore an oath—known as the Tennis Court Oath—that they would not separate from one another until the king and nobles of the Second Estate agreed to accept a constitution for France.

They were deliberately defying the king. The French Revolution was under way.

Chapter 4

A Day of Rage and Blood

On the day following the Tennis Court Oath, more than one hundred fifty clergymen, most of the delegates of the First Estate, came to join the National Assembly. A number of nobles, sincerely hoping for changes that would help the country, also joined the commoners.

On June 23, when the special meeting called by the king was held, the building where it took place was surrounded by soldiers. The king made a short speech in which he agreed to a few changes the Third Estate had asked for, such as no new taxes and greater freedom of the press. But he did not mention equality for the Third Estate, an end to privileges for the nobility, or a constitution. To end his speech, he announced that nothing would be done without his approval, and he ordered the three groups of delegates to leave and to go back to work the next day in their three separate rooms. In other words, he was commanding all the commoners, clergymen, and nobles who now formed the National Assembly, to break up and return to their original three delegations. He was refusing to recognize that a National Assembly even existed, and he had made it plain that most of the changes the commoners were hoping for were not going to be made.

Despite the king's command to leave, the members of the National Assembly remained in the hall. The nobleman who had been acting as master of ceremonies reminded them in a loud voice that they had been ordered to go. It was later said by a number of delegates that Mirabeau then stood up, and in an even louder voice, told the man, "we are here by the will of the people and we . . . will not be dispersed except at the point of bayonets!"[1]

Outside, the building was now ringed by a throng of thousands of common people. They had come from Paris, which was only twelve miles away. Fearing a riot, the officer in command of the soldiers sent to keep peace ordered them to fire into the people, to inspire terror and make the crowd break up. Just a few months earlier, before the Estates-General began, the soldiers would have obeyed. But now they knew about what the National Assembly was trying to do for commoners, and they were all commoners themselves. They refused to fire on their own people.

The king was informed that the National Assembly had ignored his command to leave the hall. "Very well, let them stay," he growled, as if he did not really care.[2] But when he learned that French soldiers were refusing to obey their officers, he grew concerned. This meant he could no longer depend on those troops. On the advice of some of his counselors, he ordered some of the army's regiments of foreign soldiers to come to Paris. These soldiers, mostly Swiss and Germans, would not refuse to fire on French commoners if ordered to do so. They could be used to make the National Assembly obey, and to break up the rowdy crowds of Paris.

A Call to Arms!

In 1789, Paris was a community of half a million people. It was then, as it still is, the main city of France. As July began, the streets of Paris became filled with surging, restless crowds of thousands of commoners. Many of them were out of work and starving. They were joined by many soldiers who were no longer willing to serve the king. These men walked about in groups, shouting such things as "Long live the Third Estate! We belong to it and will never fight, except in its defense!"[3]

Suddenly, on July 11, the king fired Necker and ordered him to leave France. He was replaced by the Baron de Breteuil, a nobleman who was known to be in favor of leaving taxes the way they were. The crowds in Paris swelled. Their mood was now ugly. A man who was their friend had been swept away and replaced by an enemy. The people felt betrayed.

In the heart of Paris was a large building known as the Royal Palace. Part of it actually was a palace, belonging to the Duke of Orleans, but much of it held shops and cafés. There was a parklike garden in the center, and people would stroll through it and visit the shops. On the afternoon of July 12, crowds were surging through the garden, seeking news. Everyone knew that King Louis had sent for foreign soldiers, and the people of Paris were fearfully expecting to be attacked.

A young man named Camille Desmoulins was standing in front of one of the cafés with some friends. He was a part-time lawyer in his twenties who had run for election as a delegate to the Estates-General but had not been selected. Desmoulins and his friends were discussing the rumors swirling through the city. Suddenly, Desmoulins could not contain himself. He leaped up onto a café table and began to speak to the crowd flowing by.

Desmoulins announced that he was calling on the people of Paris to take up weapons and fight! The German troops the king has sent for are here, he declared, and they will come into Paris tonight to butcher everyone![4] He tugged a leaf off a tree branch by his head and stuck it in his hat, urging everyone to "—take a green cockade, the color of hope—," as a symbol of their common cause.[5] Then he yanked a pistol from his pocket and brandished it in the air. "I would die rather than submit to servitude!" he yelled defiantly.[6]

Camille Desmoulins, in his twenties at the start of the revolution, stirred the people's emotions with his powerful speeches.

Desmoulins's fiery speech roused the crowd to a peak of excitement. He was cheered and hailed as a hero. People began seizing every green thing they could find and fastening it to themselves. They streamed away in all directions to spread the word of Desmoulins's speech and to search for weapons. Later in the afternoon, as Desmoulins had said would happen, there was an attack by foreign troops. A regiment of German cavalry charged into a crowd, killing an elderly man and wounding several other people.

A Search for Weapons

On the morning of July 13, the clanging of hundreds of church bells awoke Parisians as a warning of danger in the streets. Mobs were roving everywhere, searching for weapons with which to defend themselves. Some found swords and pikes, long spears that had been used by soldiers a hundred years earlier. Others broke into gunmakers' shops and helped themselves to muskets and pistols.

But swords, pikes, and a few firearms would not be enough to defend against thousands of well-armed soldiers. A fighting force was needed, not only to defend the city but to preserve order. In every part of the city, units of volunteer militia were formed—ordinary citizens willing to fight as soldiers to protect their families and neighbors. They had no uniforms, but to identify themselves they pinned circles of red and blue ribbon, the colors of the city of Paris, to their hats or coat lapels. They needed a commander, and the obvious choice was the Marquis de Lafayette. He accepted several days later, and gave these citizen soldiers the name of National Guard.

Word spread that there were thirty-two thousand muskets in the military hospital for veterans, the Invalides. Early on the morning of July 14, an immense crowd of thousands stormed the hospital and seized the muskets and a number of cannons.

However, to fire these weapons, gunpowder was needed. A musket had to have a quantity of gunpowder shoved down into the barrel, and a bullet pushed down on top of that. Someone remembered that 250 barrels of gunpowder, about 30,000 pounds, were stored at a place well-known to Parisians—the Bastille. The crowd swarmed toward it.

The Bastille was a fortress built in the 1300s and later turned into a prison. It was a huge, gloomy gray building with eight ninety-foot towers, encircled by a deep ditch that had once been a moat. For centuries, it had been a symbol of the tyranny of France's rulers. It was the object of dreadful stories of innocent people condemned to lifelong imprisonment in horrible dungeons and subjected to brutal tortures. Rumors said it was filled with prisoners, but in July 1789, there were actually only seven. Four were convicted criminals, one was an attempted murderer, and two were mentally disturbed. The Bastille's guard consisted of eighty-two crippled army veterans and thirty-two soldiers of a Swiss regiment. But the crowd that arrived

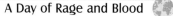

at the Bastille could see that there were cannons pointing at the street from all the towers.

The man in charge of the Bastille, the Marquis de Launay, was an elderly nobleman who simply did not know what to do when the gigantic crowd appeared and demanded that the store of gunpowder be turned over to them. He decided to stall for time, hoping that troops would show up to disperse the crowd. He offered to negotiate.

The Fall of the Bastille

A delegation of men selected by the crowd entered the Bastille to talk to de Launay. It was now ten o'clock, and he invited the men to have a late breakfast with him. De Launay seemed ready to consent to the crowd's demands and even agreed to pull the cannons on the towers back so that they could not fire. But as time dragged on, the people outside became convinced that the men they had sent in had been taken prisoner.

The mob surged forward and broke into the building's inner courtyard. Blasts of cannonfire from the towers killed eighty-three and wounded eighty-eight. Then, soldiers accompanying the crowd pushed up cannons and aimed them at the main gate. De Launay decided he had better surrender. The gate was unlocked and the drawbridge lowered. The crowd rushed into the Bastille.

In the wild scuffle that followed, six of de Launay's men were killed. Two of the men in the crowd seized

On July 14, 1789, the French Revolution began when people stormed the Bastille, demanding gunpowder stored there.

de Launay and tried to get him safely away, but another man wildly attacked him. Trying to defend himself, de Launay kicked the man, who shrieked in pain. An enraged man stabbed de Launay in the stomach with a bayonet. He fell writhing to the ground, and instantly, other members of the crowd began stabbing him with swords and bayonets and firing pistols and muskets into his body until he was dead. The man he had kicked, an unemployed cook, cut off de Launay's head with a knife, and it was stuck on the point of a pike. Holding the dripping head high, the crowd surged off in triumph. The revolution had now turned bloody. As time went on, much more blood would be spilled.

In the weeks following the storming of the Bastille, the great fortress was gradually torn down. The people of Paris did not want the hated symbol of tyranny to remain. Pieces of its stone were shaped into models of the building and turned into inkwells and other souvenirs. In time, there was nothing left of the despised prison.

The capture and destruction of the Bastille was a major symbol of the revolution. Every year thereafter, on the day the Bastille had been stormed and taken by the people of Paris, there were celebrations throughout France. To this day, July 14 is celebrated by French people everywhere, just as July 4 is celebrated by Americans. For French people, this marks the day when their freedom began.

Great Changes and a Captive King

Stunned by the storming of the Bastille, King Louis gave up his plan to regain power by using the foreign troops of his army to terrify the crowds and the delegates of the National Assembly. On July 15, he made a speech before the National Assembly, telling it he had ordered the foreign regiments to leave Paris and assuring the delegates that they were safe. The next day, he sent word to Necker to return and take his position as minister of finance again. Thus, the king had been forced to cave in completely.

When news of what had happened in Paris reached the other cities and towns of France, many of them, too, exploded into revolt. Country homes and palaces of nobles were looted and burned. Forests and lakes that had been the private hunting and fishing places of nobles were taken over by peasants. Records of debts owed to nobles by peasants were destroyed.

Many nobles now suddenly realized that they could be in terrible danger. The peasants were boiling with rage, and there was nothing to control them. It would not be long before they began murdering nobles in revenge for the harsh treatment, the toil, the taxes, and everything else they had suffered for so long. So, many nobles began to leave the country, taking as much wealth with them as they could, to settle in foreign countries. These nobles became known as *émigrés*, a French word meaning people who leave their native country because they do not like it. One of the first of the émigrés was the king's own brother, the Comte d'Artois, who left France on July 16.

The National Assembly now had the problem of trying to calm the country down and end the violence that was flaring everywhere. The Third Estate delegates did not want to send soldiers out to restore order. That would make it seem as if they were attacking the very people they represented. But the delegates who belonged to a group known as the Breton Club, which included Maximilien Robespierre, came up with a solution. Even though some of these men were wealthy nobles, they almost all believed that drastic changes were needed to save the country. What they felt had to be done was for all the nobles to give up most of their privileges, which would mean the end of feudalism in France. That would take away the cause of the peasants' rage.

While the assembly was in session on the night of August 4, two Breton Club noblemen presented the club's plan. The hall was filled with spectators, mostly Third Estate commoners. The nobles in the assembly may have been fearful of their anger. At any rate, one after another, noblemen and Church officials stood up and agreed that their privileges, which were the cause of much of the country's trouble, *should* be abolished. A few nobles objected, but it did not matter. With growing excitement, the assembly made all taxes equal for everyone, ended tithing to the Church, abolished laws protecting game animals, and virtually made all the French people equal. By the end of the night, feudalism no longer existed in France.

The March on Versailles

About three weeks later, on August 26, the assembly passed the Declaration of the Rights of Man and the Citizen. This spelled out all the freedoms that the commoners had gained and now shared with nobles and clergy. It was very much like the American Declaration of Independence and Bill of Rights. It provided the basis for a French government based on freedom of all people, under the law. This declaration had actually been written mostly by Lafayette, with the help of Thomas Jefferson, who was the American ambassador to France at this time.

Most of the country calmed down. But in Paris, where angry mobs had launched the revolution with the storming of the Bastille, there were suddenly new

Source Document

Articles:

1. Men are born and remain free and equal in rights. Social distinction may be founded only upon the general good.

2. The aim of all political association is the preservation of the natural and imprescriptible rights of man. These rights are liberty, property, security, and resistance to oppression.

3. The principle of sovereignty resides essentially in the nation. No body nor individual may exercise any authority which does not proceed directly from the nation.

4. Liberty consists in the freedom to do everything which injures no one else; hence the exercise of the natural rights of each man has no limits except those which assure to the other members of the society the enjoyment of the same rights. These limits can only be determined by law. . . .[1]

The Declaration of the Rights of Man became one of the most famous documents associated with the French Revolution.

problems. Shipments of grain to the city were very late; bread was becoming scarce and expensive; and once more, many people were going hungry. As a result, angry crowds were again beginning to appear in the streets of Paris.

Another problem was that King Louis was obviously not at all pleased about the Declaration of the Rights of Man and the loss of most of the nobility's privileges. While he stated that he approved of the "spirit" in which they had been passed, he did not ever say that he accepted them. This was cause for suspicion to begin simmering in many people's minds.

Then, something happened that brought this suspicion to a boil. On October 2, the king and queen attended a banquet along with a number of nobles and army officers. Word leaked out that nobles had shouted out insults against the assembly. It was said that many nobles pinned on white ribbons, symbols of the king, and that someone had stamped on a red and blue ribbon, symbol of the revolution. To many people, this suggested that the nobles might be preparing to try to overthrow the revolution and restore the king to power. There was talk that the king should be forced to leave Versailles and come to Paris, where an eye could be kept on him.

Paris now had a new city government, made up of common people and called the *Commune*, or "Commons." On the morning of October 5, crowds of women from all parts of Paris stormed to the City Hall, where the Commune did its work, shrieking for bread. A few men began to join them. Before long, a mob of six thousand people, mainly women, was marching toward Versailles in the pouring rain to demand that the king return to Paris and lower the price of bread. Many of the women carried swords or pikes and some had muskets. A group of them were even pulling a cannon. On the way, they smashed windows and looted shops.

They arrived in Versailles about five o'clock in the afternoon. They went first to the palace but were unable to get in. The iron gates were locked, and soldiers of two of the foreign regiments were drawn up grimly behind them. Next, the women went to the hall where the National Assembly was at work. They literally invaded it, sitting down among the delegates and demanding to see the king. They wanted the king to lower the price of bread, they explained. It was Robespierre mainly who managed to calm them down.

The King Becomes a Captive

Meanwhile, in Paris, thousands of soldiers of the National Guard were massing at the City Hall, also determined to march to Versailles. Lafayette got there on horseback as quickly as he could and tried to talk them out of it. It was no use. They wanted to get the king and bring him back to Paris. Lafayette finally gave up and agreed to lead them to Versailles.

In Versailles, the king agreed to see a few of the women. He listened to them, then announced that he would have all the bread in Versailles collected and given to them. Delighted, the women left. At eleven o'clock that night, Lafayette and the National Guard troops arrived. Lafayette sent a number of them to guard the palace. All seemed well.

But early the next morning, around five o'clock, another group of women got into the palace through a gate that had been left open. These were women known as fishwives, who sold fish in the marketplace in Paris. They lived hard lives, having to struggle to make a living. They had become tough, rude, and foul-mouthed as a result. They did not have much respect for anyone or anything, and they were not much afraid of anything. These women hated Marie Antoinette, whom they blamed for their problems. "Death to the Austrian," they shrieked, referring to the queen. ". . . tear out the heart of the *coquine* [Marie Antoinette], cut off her head, *fricasser* her liver and even then it would not be over."[2] One howled, "I'll have her kidneys in a fricassee!"[3]

Leaping out of bed, Marie Antoinette ran to the king's apartments with some of her ladies in waiting—women who were part of her personal staff. There, they huddled behind locked doors with the king and the royal children.

Lafayette, sleeping in a nearby building, was aroused and rushed to the palace. Its courtyard was now swarming with people, but the National Guard troops were blocking the entrance into the palace. Lafayette hurried to the king's rooms and talked Louis and Marie Antoinette into stepping out onto a balcony with him so the crowd could see them. Expecting to be killed, they courageously did so. There were some yells of rage, but then Lafayette bowed and kissed the queen's hand. The crowd broke into cheers, and then began to yell, "À Paris [To Paris]!"[4]

"My children, you want me to follow you back to Paris," called the king. "All right, I will, but on condition that I will not be separated from my wife and my children."[5]

That afternoon, the king, queen, their children, and many courtiers rode to Paris in carriages, surrounded by the mob of fishwives and other women. The National Guard troops marched ahead, each man with a loaf of bread stuck on his musket's bayonet.

On October 6, 1789, a mob celebrated as it forced the king to return with the people to Paris from Versailles.

Wagons full of wheat and flour trundled along in front of the procession. As they tramped through the mud of the rain-soaked road, the women chanted, "We won't lack for bread anymore! We've got the baker, the baker's wife, and the little apprentice!"[6] They seemed to believe that, as long as they had control over the king and his family, the problem of scarce bread was solved.

In Paris, the royal family was taken to a small palace, the Tuileries, where they would live, under guard, from then on. The king of France had virtually become a prisoner of the French people.

Political Clubs, Disagreements, and an Escape Attempt

The National Assembly had also returned to Paris with the king. It was now actually the government of France, and it had to solve all of France's problems. One of the many problems that still existed was that the government was nearly out of money. In November, the National Assembly solved that problem by confiscating all land owned by the Catholic Church and putting it up for sale. There was some resistance to this, especially from the clergy, but it was just the beginning of a general movement to make the Church abide by the revolution.

By the end of 1789, the delegates of the National Assembly had formed into a number of political groups with different ideas. Most of the groups set up places in various parts of Paris where they could meet to discuss their ideas and make plans. This was done in a formal way, with members standing up to give speeches in which they presented their ideas and suggestions.

One of these groups was the Breton Club, which renamed itself the Club of Friends of the Constitution. However, because its meeting place was in a building that had been a monastery of monks called Jacobins, it soon became known as the Jacobin Club. Maximilien Robespierre was still a member.

Since the National Assembly had been formed, Robespierre had often made speeches before it and taken part in all the debates and arguments about things the assembly wanted to do. He was not a very good public speaker. He had a grating, high-pitched voice and tended to use long-winded, complicated sentences. He had no flare for drama and no ability to use his voice to create excitement as speakers such as Mirabeau could. But when Robespierre made speeches about the problems of France, he spoke with such obvious sincerity about freedom and the rights of the people, that he held his listeners spellbound.

During the debates on the Declaration of the Rights of Man, Robespierre made several important speeches. In August, he spoke against any restrictions on what could be written in books or newspapers, saying that freedom of the press went hand-in-hand with freedom of speech. In December, he made a speech demanding equal rights for three groups of people who did not have them—Jews, Protestants, and actors, most of whom then were little more than vagabonds, without permanent homes. These people were all French citizens, Robespierre pointed out, and they deserved the rights that all other citizens had.

However, Robespierre did not convince many of the other delegates to adopt his opinions. He seemed too radical for most of them, too much in favor of tremendous changes that would make the country totally different. Most of the members of the assembly did not want to get rid of the king. They merely wanted to reduce his powers. But they sensed that Robespierre actually wanted to end the rule of a king in France.

Many Differences of Opinion

Robespierre showed up at the Jacobin Club almost every evening and often gave speeches about his revolutionary ideas. The Marquis de Lafayette and some of his followers were also members of the club, but they did not share Robespierre's views. Still, Robespierre became a great favorite of most of the other members. In March 1790, they elected him the club's president. Under Robespierre's leadership, other Jacobin clubs, whose members shared the beliefs and ideas of the Paris club, were set up throughout most of France.

In April, Camille Desmoulins and a few others organized another club. It, too, had an old monastery as its meeting place. It was known as the Cordeliers Club, from the name of the area of Paris where the building was located.

The Cordeliers were fiery radical revolutionaries who wanted to do away with the king and turn France into a republic, like the United States. Among their members were two men regarded as the most violent revolutionaries in France, who believed the revolution would only succeed if all its enemies were wiped out. Jean Paul Marat, born in Switzerland, ran a newspaper called *The Friend of the People*, for which he wrote editorials that helped spread his ideas. Georges Jacques Danton was a successful lawyer in Paris and a skillful speaker who could excite people with his words.

Thus, from the beginning of 1790, it was clear that there were deep differences of opinion among the leaders of the revolution. The Cordeliers and some of the Jacobins wanted a republic. Mirabeau, Lafayette, and others wanted a constitutional monarchy—with Louis as king but ruling according to strict laws set down in a constitution. The followers of the Duke of Orleans also wanted a constitutional monarchy but with Orleans as king. And there were still nobles, lurking undercover, who wanted to restore France to the way it had been before the revolution began, with Louis as an all-powerful king and with all their privileges restored.

A shattering blow was struck against these nobles in June 1790. The National Assembly voted to abolish all nobility in France, making nobles the equals of everyone else. There were to be no more dukes, counts, or barons. From now on, everyone—from a

Source Document

From this moment the French nation proclaims the sovereignty of the people, the suppression of all civil and military authorities which have hitherto governed you and all of the taxes which you bear, under whatever form, the abolition of the tithe, of feudalism, of seigniorial rights and monopolies of every kind, of serfdom, whether real or personal, of hunting and fishing privileges, of the corvee, the salt tax, the tolls and local imposts, and, in general, of all various kinds of taxes with which you have been loaded by your usurpers; it also proclaims the abolition among you of all noble and ecclesiastical corporations and of all prerogatives and privileges opposed to equality. You are, from this moment, brothers and friends; all are citizens, equal in rights, and all are alike called to govern, to serve, and to defend your country.[1]

The National Assembly made some sweeping changes when it took charge of the French government during the revolution.

former marquis to a ragged ditchdigger—would be addressed simply as "Citizen."

On July 12, the National Assembly passed an act designed to force the clergy into equality with the rest of the people. Known as the Civil Constitution of the Clergy, this act abolished all Catholic convents and monasteries and turned all members of the clergy into civil servants, paid by the government. It also ordered that bishops and archbishops be elected by vote instead of being appointed by the king.

The Flight of the Royal Family

Some months later, the pope announced that he would not allow these changes, and that any priest or nun who accepted them would be excommunicated, or expelled from the Church. Of course, most French priests and bishops also refused to abide by the changes. In November, to try and force the clergy to accept the changes, the assembly passed a decree demanding that all clergy take an oath of loyalty to the constitution. More than half the clergy refused, and thousands of their parishioners backed them. On the other hand, many thousands of people began to demonstrate against the Catholic Church.

In the midst of all this, Mirabeau died on April 2, at the age of forty-three. It was said that his last words were that the monarchy was also going to die, and that many groups would fight for its remains. That seemed to be exactly what was happening. By the spring of

1791, France was again torn by disagreement and dissent.

Lafayette's group in the National Assembly was rushing to finish the writing of a constitution, in hopes that it would finally bring all the turmoil and violence to an end. But now, the nobles who wanted a return to the old ways struck a blow, with an attempt to help the king and his family escape from France.

On the night of June 21, Louis and his family, including his sister Elizabeth, entered a coach driven by a disguised nobleman and left Paris. The royal family was disguised as servants. Louis was dressed in cheap commoner clothing. He carried identification papers that said he was a valet, a servant who takes care of a man's clothing and helps him make a good appearance. The queen was costumed as a governess, or "nanny," a woman who takes care of children. The thirteen-year-old princess and the six-year-old prince were both dressed in girls' clothing. The Comte de Provence and his wife, also disguised, were in another coach, but taking a different road.

Their plan was to go to the town of Montmedy on the border of the Austrian Netherlands (now Belgium) and cross the border to safety. It was their belief that Marie Antoinette's brother, Emperor Leopold, would eventually provide them with an Austrian Army. Louis would accompany that army back into France in an invasion that, he hoped, would destroy the revolution and put him back in full power.

The Comte de Provence and his wife made it across the border. But for the royal family, things went wrong. In the morning, the coach was held up for hours by a broken wheel, and the soldiers who were supposed to have met the king to protect him did not arrive. Then, as the carriage passed through the town of St. Menehould late in the day, a man recognized the king from his picture on France's paper money. This man, Jean-Baptiste Drouet, was an ardent patriot who believed firmly in the revolution. He felt that, if the king were trying to sneak out of France in disguise, it could only be part of a plot to destroy what the revolution had accomplished.

Recapture and Disgrace

Drouet had once been a dragoon, a soldier of a cavalry regiment, so he was a skillful horseman. Flinging himself onto a horse, he galloped up a side road at breakneck speed to the next town, Varennes. There, he alerted the town officials that King Louis of France was going to try to pass through their town in an attempt to leave the country.

When the coach carrying Louis and his family reached Varennes, at about eleven-thirty that night, it was brought to a stop by a crowd of townspeople with torches and muskets, and a group of town officials. The officials were not quite sure what to do. They had only Drouet's word that the chubby man who said he was a valet was actually the king. Then, someone remembered that there was an elderly man living in the town who had lived in Versailles for many years and had often seen the king. Surely, he would be able to determine if the valet named Durand were really Louis XVI.

The man was sent for. When his eyes fell upon Louis, he automatically knelt, as commoners had always done in the presence of the king. Louis sighed. Realizing he could no longer hide his true identity. "I am indeed your King."[2]

Four days later, Louis and his family returned to Paris under guard, passing through crowds that shouted, "Long live the nation! Long live the National Assembly!"[3] Only a few weeks earlier, they would have been shouting, "Long live the king" at the sight of Louis. But now, whatever respect the king had left had been wiped out by his attempt to flee the country. Representatives of the National Assembly coldly told Louis he would no longer be regarded as king until he accepted the constitution.

Most of the members of the assembly still wanted France to be a constitutional monarchy, with a king. But outside the assembly, many people felt that the king should be tried and punished in some way for his attempt to leave France. And many more, especially the poorest working people, wanted the king to be removed and France to be a republic. Danton, Marat, and the rest of the Cordeliers Club did everything they could to make that idea spread. Robespierre and many of the Jacobins also began to speak loudly in favor of a republic. Slowly, the monarchists and the republicans began to regard each other as enemies.

On July 17, something happened that brought a confrontation between the two groups. At a park in Paris, members of the Cordeliers Club led by Camille Desmoulins set up a big meeting of people who wanted France to become a republic. Thousands attended, mostly working people. During the meeting, two men were discovered in a hiding place, and people began to shout that they were monarchist spies. Enraged, the crowd hanged them.

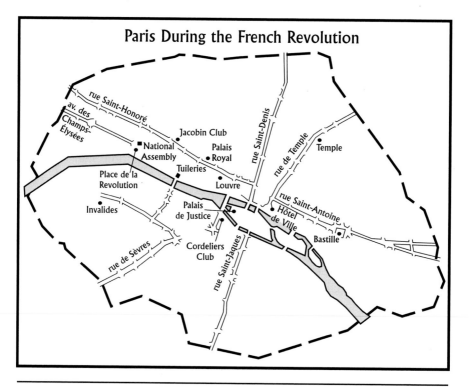

Many of the sites associated with the French Revolution can be seen on this map of Paris, as it looked during the years of the revolution.

The Triumph of the Monarchists

Word of this quickly reached the city hall. Fearing a riot, the mayor ordered Lafayette to take some National Guard troops to the park and break up the crowd. Reaching the park, Lafayette called out to the people to leave and go home. He was jeered and booed, and the crowd began to throw stones at the soldiers.

The soldiers opened fire. Fifty people went down, and the rest began to run. Lafayette may or may not have given the actual command to fire, but from this time on, Robespierre obviously hated him. When Danton heard what had happened, he exclaimed, "If Lafayette has fired on the people, he's done for! Those who drink the people's blood die of it!"[4] Danton, too, became Lafayette's enemy.

The monarchists in control of the assembly now saw their chance to crush the republican movement. Under the pretense of preventing riots and lawlessness, they ordered the Cordeliers Club closed. Marat's newspaper and several others that supported the republican movement were shut down. An order went out for the arrest of Camille Desmoulins and others. All members of the Jacobin Club who were monarchists left the club, making it only about half as large as it had been. Despite this, Robespierre managed to hold the club together.

The republicans saw that they were in serious danger. Desmoulins and Marat went into hiding. Danton left France and went to England. Robespierre was convinced by a friend, Maurice Duplay, to leave the apartment where he was living and move secretly into Duplay's home.

Many of the monarchists who had left the Jacobin Club were members of the National Assembly. They, and others who believed as they did, formed a group that became known as the Feuillants. This, too, was a name that came from a religious order of monks.

The Feuillants now had control. In September, the constitution was finished as they wanted it. It preserved the monarchy and kept Louis as king, although with far less power than he had once had. It spelled out a great many things that he could no longer do. However, it did give him one important power—he could veto, or block, any law the assembly might try to pass that he did not like. On September 14, at a special ceremony, Louis swore to accept the constitution, and thus once more officially became king of the French people.

The National Assembly prepared to close itself down. Preparations began for the election of a new assembly that would govern France under the constitution. Most people believed that the revolution was now over.

They were wrong.

Chapter 7

A War and the Downfall of the King

On the next-to-last day before the National Assembly closed down, one of the Feuillants, a man named Isaac Le Chapelier, stood up and proposed the passage of a new law. Because political clubs such as the Jacobins and Cordeliers had caused so much trouble, he said, they should be controlled by the government. He proposed that any attempt by a club to criticize the government, to criticize members of the assembly, or to have its members speak before large crowds should be against the law. Now that the revolution was over, Le Chapelier stated, the clubs no longer had any purpose and could only cause trouble.

Before Le Chapelier finished speaking, Robespierre stood up and challenged him. Robespierre charged that what Le Chapelier was suggesting would not only destroy the clubs but also do away with some of the basic rights that were in the constitution—freedom of speech, freedom of assembly, and freedom of the press. He declared that the revolution was not over as long as there were still people in France who wanted to return to the old ways of absolute monarchy. He showed how, with laws such as Le Chapelier was proposing, those enemies could gain strength and end liberty. Then, just as American patriot Patrick Henry had said, "Give me liberty, or give me death!" Robespierre exclaimed, "Let me perish myself before the death of liberty!"[1]

Thousands of spectators heard Robespierre's speech, and it made him a hero. Word of the speech swept through Paris. The next day, when the National Assembly came to an end, a huge crowd carried Robespierre triumphantly out of the hall on its shoulders.

Robespierre had become a tremendous favorite of the people. Both his supporters and those who disliked him agreed that he was an absolutely sincere and honest man. He could have become a millionaire by using his position in the government to do favors for people who would pay him for his help. Many politicians were doing this. But Robespierre utterly refused to do such things. He had become known as the Incorruptible, meaning a person who could not be bribed, or corrupted, for any amount.

There seems no doubt that Robespierre sincerely believed that a politician had to *be* incorruptible. He lived on nothing more than the salary he was given as a member of the assembly. He ate meager meals of bread, fruit, and coffee. Like most French people, he drank wine with his meals, but he watered it down a great deal. He did not have a girlfriend, and for amusement, he generally just went for walks in a park or sometimes went to a play. The only thing in which he seemed really interested was trying to make the revolution succeed.

The Girondins Hatch a Plot

On October 1, the newly elected government, known as the Legislative (lawmaking) Assembly, held its first meeting. The delegates were all men who had not been members of the National Assembly, because by law, those men could not serve two terms in a row. Of the new delegates, 136 were Jacobins, 264 were Feuillants, and 400 were not committed to any group.

The different groups began sitting together, each in a precise place, with the Feuillants on the right, the uncommitted delegates in the middle, and the Jacobins on the left. Thus, the idea of political positions was born. To this day, conservative politicians who do not believe in change are said to belong to the right, liberals who want great changes are said to be on the left, and moderates who do not side with either the right or left are said to be in the center.

One of the new delegates was Jacques Brissot. He led a small but very active group of delegates who were all members of the Jacobin Club. This group was known as the Girondins, because most of them came from a district of France known as the Gironde. The Girondins often met in the home of one of their members, Jean-Marie Roland, and his beautiful, intelligent wife, Madame Manon Roland. Working through her husband, Madame Roland actually gave the Girondins a lot of their ideas.

Like most Jacobins, the Girondins wanted to get rid of the king and make France a republic. Led by Brissot, they started a campaign designed to make the king—and the Feuillants—look bad.

They did this by forcing the king to use the veto against things that most people were in favor of. It was well-known that many of the émigré nobles were trying to talk some of the rulers of nearby countries into invading France, to help restore Louis to full power. So, on November 9, with the help of many of the uncommitted delegates, the Girondins managed to pass a decree ordering all émigrés to return to France. Of course, Louis could not allow such a decree to pass. Any émigré who returned would probably be executed or at least imprisoned. Two of the émigrés were the king's own brothers. He vetoed the decree.

Next, the Girondins managed to push through a decree that punished all Catholic priests who had not taken the oath to obey the constitution. It took away their pensions and forced them to leave the places where they were working. Louis was a staunch Catholic. He was appalled by the decree, and vetoed it, too.

Girondin Victory and a Move Toward War

As the Girondins had hoped, the king's popularity dropped sharply. Among the common working people he was called "Monsieur Veto."

A number of the uncommitted delegates of the assembly now joined the Girondins and Jacobins. The Feuillants were no longer the most powerful group in the assembly. By the end of 1791, the Girondins, also known as Brissotins, were in control. By March 1792, they were even able to force the king to dismiss the last of his noble ministers and appoint ministers who were favorable to the Girondins. Jean-Marie Roland became minister of the interior; Georges Jacques Danton became minister of justice; Charles François Dumouriez, a general, was named minister of foreign affairs. Part of Dumouriez's job was to get things ready in case of war, and this was important to the Girondins.

The Girondins wanted a war. They believed that the revolution was in grave danger from several foreign countries. In August 1791, the Austrian emperor and the king of Prussia (a small but powerful German kingdom) had issued a proclamation declaring that it was the duty of all European monarchs to help restore the king of France to his former power. In other words, they were urging the rulers of European nations to send armies to invade France, restore the king to full power, and destroy everything the revolution had accomplished. Accordingly, the Girondins

The Departments of France
During the Revolution
1789–1799

During the early years of the revolution, France was divided into departments for better government.

believed that, instead of waiting to be attacked, France should attack first and declare war on Austria and Prussia.

The Girondins were not the only ones who wanted war. Lafayette and the Feuillants believed that a war could help them restore the idea of a constitutional monarchy. The king was also in favor of war, because he thought a war might restore him to full power. However, he pretended to believe as the Girondins did, that a war was necessary to protect France.

One of the few people who did not want war was Maximilien Robespierre. He was mainly against the idea of war because he saw clearly that it might help the king and destroy the revolution. He was also afraid that, during a war, it would be easy for some general, such as Lafayette, who had been put in charge of one of the armies, to seize power over France. The National Assembly had voted that its members could not serve in the new Legislative Assembly, so Robespierre could not speak there. But he could still argue his beliefs in the Jacobin Club, and he continued to do so. His main opponent was Brissot, and for more than two months, the two men spent many nights at the Jacobin Club, debating about the war.

Robespierre Argues Against War

Brissot believed a war would end the danger that foreign countries might invade France. He felt sure that French armies would be able to conquer their opponents. Robespierre was not sure of this at all. He was afraid that France was in no shape to go to war. It was still badly in need of money, food was still scarce, and the army was in bad condition. Most of the officers were gone. Six thousand of them had been nobles and had become émigrés. Most of the foreign regiments were also gone. France's new army was mainly made up of poorly equipped, untrained, and inexperienced men.

Brissot also seemed to believe that it was France's duty to try to bring the idea of the revolution to other countries. He felt that France's soldiers should be "armed missionaries," helping liberate the poor and peasants of other countries as the poor and peasants of France had been liberated. He spoke of the war as a "new crusade."[2]

Robespierre scoffed at this. He pointed out that no one liked people who tried to impose their ideas by force. The people the "armed missionaries" tried to convert would end up fighting them, Robespierre warned.[3]

In time, it became obvious that Robespierre had lost the debate. On April 20, 1792, the king went before the assembly and made a speech, announcing, "I have now come . . . to propose war—"[4] He received thunderous applause and cheers. Burning with excitement, the assembly voted to declare war on Austria, which was generally regarded as France's main enemy.

In those days, battles were fought by armies formed of groups of seven hundred to a thousand men, called battalions. They marched with machinelike precision and fired their muskets all at once, in volleys that hurled hundreds of bullets at the enemy in a single blast as deadly as a modern machine gun's. To fight in this fashion took training, discipline, and experience. In their first encounter with the well-disciplined, well-equipped Austrian battalions in the Austrian Netherlands (Belgium), the ragged, poorly trained, and inexperienced French troops simply turned and ran. Robespierre had been right.

The king soon found that he could not get along with his Girondin ministers. On June 10, he dismissed them all. He appointed a number of Feuillants to take their place.

As the war continued to go badly and as the money and food problems grew worse, the French people became angry and violent. Because the noblemen of the Second Estate wore a type of knee-length breeches known as *culottes*, most workingmen were now wearing long trousers, to show that they opposed the nobles. They had become known as *sans-culottes*, or "without breeches." Throughout the country, crowds of sans-culottes were rioting, setting fire to castles that had belonged to nobles, and even murdering people they suspected of being against the revolution.

The Invasion of the Tuileries

On June 20, the people who had believed the revolution was over learned how wrong they were. At three o'clock in the afternoon, a mob of eight thousand sans-culottes of Paris, including women and children,

Cartoons like this one, showing people supporting the revolution by carrying the heads of their enemies on poles, became common during the French Revolution, as the people grew more violent.

stormed to the palace of the Tuileries. They intended to force the king to take back the ministers he had dismissed and stop using the veto. They were armed with clubs, axes, pikes, and a few muskets. A group of them was pulling a cannon along by ropes. The National Guard soldiers guarding the palace simply threw down their muskets and moved out of the way. The sansculottes surged into the palace. It was a hot, muggy day. Most of them were dirty and they probably smelled. Many were drunk. They began to smash furniture and chop down doors with axes. There were shouts of "Down with the veto!"[5]

They broke into a small room and found Louis standing there, waiting for them. It was a brave thing to do, because he probably expected to be murdered. One man did lunge at him with a sword but was pulled back by others. Louis spoke to them with a great deal of dignity and courage, asking them what they wanted. To humiliate him, the sans-culottes made him put on a red stocking cap, a symbol of the revolution, and made him drink a toast to the success of the revolution. This seemed to calm them down. Then the mayor of Paris appeared and urged them to leave peaceably. After a time, they did, triumphantly slouching out of the palace, grinning and chuckling over their triumph.

Word of this trickled out of Paris and eventually reached the headquarters of the commander of the Prussian Army, the Duke of Brunswick. A nobleman, the duke was enraged to hear of such treatment of a king. In his anger, he did a rather foolish thing. In late July, he sent the people of Paris a message. He threatened to destroy the entire city if the king and royal family were harmed.

For the sans-culottes, this was nothing less than proof that the king was secretly communicating with the enemies of France. Stirred up by the writings of the fiery Marat in his newspaper *The Friend of the People*, a gigantic mob of twenty thousand sans-culottes marched to the Tuileries on the morning of August 10.

The royal family could hear a distant roaring sound growing ever louder, the noise of the approaching mob.

This antirevolutionary cartoon shows one of the sans-culottes dancing in joy amid the violence and death of the revolution.

The king and his family fled from the palace and sought protection from the Legislative Assembly. At the Tuileries, there was a battle between the mob and the Swiss Guard Regiment that was now guarding the palace and had sworn to protect the king. The soldiers were brutally wiped out—shot, stabbed, clubbed to death, hacked to pieces with axes. Several hundred sans-culottes also lost their lives.

The End of the Monarchy

The assembly had Louis and his family put under guard in an old medieval castle known as the Temple Prison. They were under the supervision of the government of the city of Paris, the Commune. Many of the members of the Commune were men who had stormed the Bastille and attacked the Tuileries. They had no liking for the royal family.

Louis had been deposed—removed from power. He was no longer acknowledged as king. The monarchy was over. The revolution had been started by the bourgeoisie, the middle-class members of the National Assembly, most of whom wanted a constitutional monarchy. Now, it had been taken over by the sans-culottes, the working people and the poor, who wanted an end to kings. France was now to be a democracy, a government of the people.

The Birth of a Republic, the Death of a King

With the monarchy abolished, General Lafayette knew he was in danger because he was a monarchist. When the Austrian and Prussian forces invaded France on August 19, 1792, Lafayette surrendered to them in order to save himself. The Legislative Assembly declared him a traitor, and General Dumouriez was appointed to take command of his army.

It was obvious that the assembly, which had been formed mainly to create a constitutional-monarchy type of government, was no longer of any use, since a constitutional monarchy was now impossible. A new constitution and a new government were needed. The assembly set up an election with which a new government could be formed.

On September 2, the important fortress city of Verdun was taken by the Prussians. Verdun was only one hundred fifty miles straight up the road from Paris. It was clear that the Prussian forces were marching straight toward Paris, and everyone remembered the Duke of Brunswick's threat. Driven by fear and rage, mobs of sans-culottes stormed through Paris, murdering anyone they decided was an enemy of the revolution. They broke into all the prisons, where many people accused of working against the revolution had been sent—nobles, monarchists, priests who refused to sign the oath to the constitution. Most of these people, nearly fourteen hundred persons, were simply butchered, often in horrible ways. A man walking near one of the prisons while this was going on later wrote that the gutter leading from the building was actually flowing with blood![1]

Most of the working people of Paris were in favor of these massacres. They had been living in terror that the monarchists in the prisons might break out and start slaughtering *them*. Many of the Jacobins were also in favor of the massacres, believing they were cleansing France of those who were against the revolution. But the Girondins opposed the massacres, insisting they were a threat to law and order. A rift began to grow between the two groups. The Jacobins were clearly on the side of the sans-culottes and poor working people, but the Girondins had shown that they seemed to favor the wealthy, "upper-class" bourgeoisie.

On September 20, in an astounding victory, the French Army, led by Dumouriez, managed to halt the advance of the Prussian force moving toward Paris.

The Prussian commander, the Duke of Brunswick, ordered a retreat all the way out of France. The threat against Paris was over.

One day later, the first meeting of the new government, the National Convention, began in Paris. Among the members were 110 Jacobins, including Robespierre, Marat, Danton, and Desmoulins. Around 200 Girondins, including Brissot, had also been voted in. The rest of the 440 members were not committed to any particular point of view. Among the Girondins there was one foreigner—American Thomas Paine, who had been a tremendous force in the American Revolution. As a noted revolutionary, he had been granted French citizenship.

Treason and a Trial

The Jacobins sat at the left, in an area that happened to be higher than the rest of the hall. Because of this, they became known as the Mountain. Their leader, who planned most of what they did, was Robespierre.

The uncommitted delegates sat in a broad group in the center and were soon known as the Plain, and sometimes as the Swamp. The Girondins had now become the party of the right—"right-wing" conservatives. Their leader was still Brissot.

The first issue the convention took up was the kind of government France should now have. The decision was unanimous. The monarchy was abolished. No more kings! France was now a republic—a nation in which the government is a group of citizens elected to vote for what they feel the majority of the nation's citizens want. September 22 was announced as the first day of Year One of the Republic.

Almost at once, the Jacobins began demanding a trial for the former king. Some Jacobins wanted him executed as a traitor. On December 3, Robespierre stood up to speak. In a speech that became famous, he argued that a trial was not even necessary, because Louis had already been judged guilty by the *people*.[2] The people were the final judges, said Robespierre. He slyly asked a trick question—if the king were tried and found innocent despite the judgment of the people, would that not seem to mean that the people and the revolution were wrong? Such a possibility had to be prevented from happening. Robespierre urged that Louis simply be brought before the convention and sentenced to death.

Most of the Girondins did not want to see the king executed. Brissot made a speech in which he asked if it were really necessary for a man to die in order to end the monarchy.[3] Thomas Paine, the American, also argued against executing the king. He urged that Louis be sent to America, to live out the rest of his life there.[4] The Girondins did everything they could to prevent a trial of the king.

But then, actual evidence was discovered that Louis had indeed been doing things to try to damage the revolution. A workman making repairs in the Tuileries had found a metal box hidden in a wall. It contained copies of many letters and documents, all signed by the king, revealing that he had been dealing with many people who were known to be against the revolution.

The discovery of the evidence ended opposition to a trial. In December, Louis was put on trial for treason. Because the first king of France had been a man named Hugh Capet, the former King Louis was now formally known as Citizen Louis Capet. He was allowed to select two lawyers to help defend him. For days, he was questioned by members of the convention.

A Sentence of Death

On January 15, the convention took a vote to determine whether Louis were guilty of conspiracy against the republic. All the deputies present voted yes.

The vote to decide Louis's punishment began at eight o'clock on the evening of January 16. Marat had demanded that each delegate should give his vote aloud, so that everyone could tell exactly where he stood. One by one, the delegates marched up to the platform. Some said only a single word, some made a few remarks. The convention hall was crowded with hundreds of spectators, who watched all this as if it were a play, drinking wine and brandy and eating oranges.

The voting came to an end at nine the next morning. There had been 321 votes for various kinds of imprisonment, but 394 for death. So, under majority rule, Louis had been sentenced to die. On Sunday, January 20, the convention set his execution for the next day. That night, he and his wife and children spent several hours together in a last tearful good-bye.

For hundreds of years, there had been two kinds of executions—one for commoners and one for nobles. Commoners were hanged—a slow, painful death by strangling. Nobles were beheaded with an axe—generally a quick, painless death. But now all Frenchmen were equal and were executed in the same way—by guillotine.

This was a device named after National Assembly delegate Dr. Joseph Ignace Guillotin. It was a machine for quickly and efficiently cutting off a person's head. Guillotin had hoped that such a machine would be a humane, painless way to execute criminals.

At eight-thirty Monday morning, Louis was taken to the guillotine. It stood on a platform in the middle of an enormous open square known as the Place of the Revolution, just about in the center of Paris. (Today, this is known as the Place de la Concorde—the "Place of Harmony.") People sentenced to death by guillotine were generally taken to it in a horse-drawn wooden cart known as a tumbrel, but Louis went in a carriage, with cavalrymen riding in front and behind. When the carriage arrived, Louis stepped out and climbed the wooden stairs that led to the top of the platform and the guillotine. Twenty thousand people packed the square around the platform.

The Execution of Citizen Louis Capet

The executioners quickly and skillfully cut Louis's hair short, so that his neck was bare for the blade. Louis

On the night before his execution, Louis XVI spent some intimate moments, saying good-bye to his children and his wife.

argued angrily for a moment when they started to tie his hands, then relaxed and let them do what they had to.

Louis tried to say some last words to the crowd, but the officer in charge of the soldiers quickly ordered the fifteen drummers to beat a steady roll that drowned out his voice. Those closest thought that the former king had declared he was innocent of the crimes he had been accused of, and that he hoped the shedding of his blood would not cause any misfortune for France.[5]

Then he knelt down and lay flat on the plank that was pushed forward so that his neck was directly below the blade. The executioner cut the cord.

Most accounts of the execution say simply that the blade plummeted down and the king's head fell. But one report states that Louis's neck was so very fat that Dr. Guillotin's painless and humane machine did not work properly. According to this account, the blade fell and the former king screamed, because his neck had not been cut through. It was said that a second try was needed, and this time it was successful.

When it was over, one of the guards picked up Louis's head and walked around the guillotine, holding the head high for everyone to see. There was a moment of silence, then the crowd began to give shouts of "Long live the republic!" A great deal of blood had spurted from the king's body and formed droplets and puddles around the bottom of the guillotine. People surged forward and began to dab this up with bits of cloth and paper and handkerchiefs. They wanted souvenirs of the historic event. After a time, the crowd began to break up and leave. There was much laughter and shouts of gaiety, as if the people were rejoicing. Some of them even joined hands and danced around the guillotine.

Marie Antoinette and the young prince were sitting at the breakfast table when the king died, but they were not eating. Suddenly, there was a boom of cannons in the distance. Through the window, they heard the soldiers on guard duty, shouting, "Long live the republic!" The queen and prince realized that Louis was dead, and they burst into tears.

Although with his famous speech Maximilien Robespierre had probably done more than anyone to have the king executed, he was not among the crowd that watched the execution and celebrated afterward. He spent the day in his room in the Duplay house, and asked the Duplays to keep the window shutters closed all day. One of the young Duplay girls asked him why. He told her, "Because there is something that is going to take place today that it is not seemly that you should see."[6]

Citizen Louis Capet's body, with his head in a basket between his legs, was taken to a Paris cemetery. It was put into a cheap wooden coffin, which was covered with quicklime, a dissolving chemical, and buried ten feet deep. Years later, when the body was dug up for reburial, there was nothing left but an earthy sludge.

Chapter 9

Civil War, a Trial, and a Murder

The execution of the former king stunned Europe. To show its disapproval, the British government ordered the French ambassador to leave England. In retaliation, the Girondin leader, Brissot, demanded that France declare war on Great Britain as well as its ally, the Dutch Republic. A short time later, war was also declared on Spain. France was now at war with six European nations. To provide soldiers, Brissot urged the convention to approve a national conscription— forced service in the army for all men in the country. This was done on February 1, 1793. Three hundred thousand men were drafted into the army.

For a time, the French armies were victorious. French troops invaded Germany and captured the city of Frankfurt. Nice and Savoy, possessions of the Italian Kingdom of Sardinia, where Louis's sister was

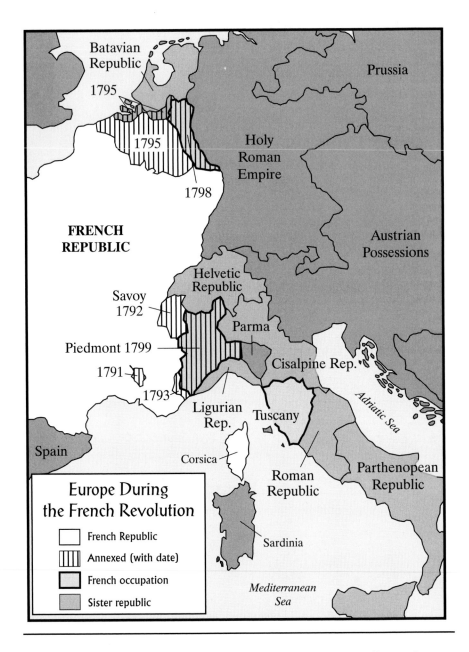

Batavian
Republic

1795

Prussia

1795

1798

Holy
Roman
Empire

FRENCH
REPUBLIC

Austrian
Possessions

Helvetic
Republic

Savoy
1792

Parma

Piedmont 1799

Cisalpine Rep.

1791

Adriatic Sea

1793

Ligurian
Rep.

Tuscany

Spain

Corsica

Roman
Republic

Parthenopean
Republic

**Europe During
the French Revolution**

☐ French Republic

▦ Annexed (with date)

▨ French occupation

▩ Sister republic

Sardinia

Mediterranean
Sea

*During the revolution, France went to war to expand its influence in
Europe. For a time, the war went well. Some of the territories it
occupied, or considered "sister republics," can be seen here.*

queen, were captured and made part of France. General Dumouriez's army advanced deep into Belgium.

Then, things suddenly turned around. Dumouriez was defeated by an Austrian army and had to fall back. He blamed this on the French government's inability to provide him with enough money, equipment, and trained soldiers. He issued a proclamation charging that the revolution had ruined France, and began making preparations to lead his army back to Paris. He intended to destroy the convention and set up a new monarchy. When he found that his soldiers would not stand for such an attempt to end the revolution, Dumouriez left his army and turned himself over to the Austrians, as Lafayette had done.

Dumouriez was, of course, condemned as a traitor by the convention. Because he had been on the Girondins' side for so long, the Jacobins began to accuse them of coddling traitors. A number of members of the Plain now joined the Jacobins, and the Girondins' power began to slip away.

In March, in the region of France known as the Vendée, open rebellion broke out as the people refused to obey the conscription law. The Vendée peasants were mostly staunch Catholics and firm monarchists, and they would not be put into the army of a government that had killed their king and tried to destroy their religion. There were also similar uprisings in other places. Units of French soldiers were sent to put down these uprisings and found themselves fighting armies of peasants. Thus, there was now civil war in France—people of the same nation in armed conflict with each other.

To try to regain control, the convention set up a group of judges and lawyers called the Revolutionary Tribunal, to judge all activities against the revolution. The penalty for such activities was death. Several days later, on April 6, a nine-man group known as the Committee of Public Safety was also formed. It had control over the entire convention, deciding what laws should be made, raising and provisioning armies, and determining who would be arrested for treason. Most of the men picked for the committee were neither Jacobins nor Girondins, but one of them was Georges Danton.

The Downfall of the Girondins

A new small group of revolutionaries had appeared among the sans-culottes. Known as the Enraged Ones, they charged that there were men making money off the poor by holding back food to make the prices go up. Furthermore, they declared that these enemies of the people were being secretly protected by the Girondins. On March 9 and 10, groups of Enraged Ones made anti-Girondin demonstrations, smashing the presses of two Girondin newspapers.

The Girondins quickly made a desperate move to try to regain their power and stop any more attacks on them. Marat, who was now president of the Jacobin Club, had been bitterly attacking them in his newspaper, so they launched an attempt to eliminate him. They accused him of being linked to the Enraged Ones, and of trying to destroy the revolution with "dangerous and radical" ideas. They urged that he should be brought to trial and expelled from the convention. With Marat out of the way, there would be less opposition to the Girondins' activities.

But their plan backfired. Marat was extremely popular among the sans-culottes of Paris, and huge crowds began to gather around the convention building, showing support for him. When Marat came to trial, he defended himself vigorously and was finally judged not guilty. The convention was invaded by sans-culottes, who carried Marat about triumphantly on their shoulders.

The Girondins did not give up. They demanded an investigation of the sans-culottes and the arrest of their leaders. They charged that the convention was in danger from these people, and urged that it be moved from Paris, for its safety.

With the help of Robespierre, Marat, and the Jacobins, the Commune and the sans-culottes organized a major attack on the Girondins. On the morning of June 2, representatives of the Commune came to the convention and demanded the arrest of the Girondin leaders. The hall was packed with sans-culottes, and there was a tumult of shouts and threats in support of the demand. While Robespierre and the Jacobins of the Mountain silently and stolidly sat where they were, the badly frightened Girondins and

Marat was one of the most popular leaders of the French Revolution among the sans-culottes. They were infuriated when Marat was attacked by the Girondins.

the delegates of the Plain tried to leave the hall. However, they found the building surrounded by thousands of National Guard troops and sans-culottes, with dozens of cannons pointing toward the doors. The commander of the soldiers coldly demanded that the Girondins be arrested.

The delegates hurried back inside. Marat stood up among the Jacobins and asked to speak. He read off a list of the names of twenty-nine Girondins. Georges Couthon, a Jacobin who was one of Robespierre's strongest supporters, made a motion that these men be expelled from the convention. Giving in completely, the convention voted to accept the motion. Brissot and the other Girondin leaders were led from the hall, under arrest. The Girondins were through as a political force, and the Mountain and the Jacobins were now in complete control.

The Murder of Marat

In Normandy, a northern area of France, lived a twenty-five-year-old woman named Charlotte Corday. She believed that the ideas of the Girondins were the only hope for the success of the revolution, and that Marat and the Jacobins would destroy everything. In July, she left her home and went to Paris. She had only one reason for going there—she intended to kill Jean Paul Marat, in order to save the revolution.

At seven o'clock on the night of July 12, she made her way into Marat's house. She called out that she had special information for Marat, about traitors in

Normandy. Hearing her, he called to his servant to let her in.

Corday entered the room where Marat was at work writing. Marat suffered from a horrible skin disease. At times, he could get relief from the itching and burning only by immersing his body in water mixed with vinegar and certain chemicals. He was seated in a high bathtub, with only his head, shoulders, and arms above the water. A board was placed across the top of the tub, on which he could do his writing. He and Corday talked for a while, then she began to give him a list of the supposed traitors. As he bent over to begin writing the names, the woman slid a knife out of her dress and stabbed him savagely in the chest. With blood pouring from his body, Marat yelled for help. Charlotte Corday did not attempt to run away, but simply walked calmly out of the room. Marat's servant leaped at the woman, knocking her to the floor and holding her there.

Marat's lung had been punctured, and he quickly died. When news of this swept through Paris, there was a tremendous surge of grief among the poor and working people. When time came for his burial, immense crowds followed the coffin through the streets. In Paris, several streets were renamed in his honor, and a number of towns throughout France were also renamed for him.

Charlotte Corday was tried in a court of law for murder and found guilty. On July 19, she went to the guillotine. Before putting her neck beneath the blade,

An artist depicted the arrest of Charlotte Corday, the assassin of Jean Paul Marat.

she cried out, "I killed one man in order to save a hundred thousand!"[1]

Georges Danton had not been doing his job well, and on July 20, Danton and one of his friends were removed from the Committee of Public Safety. Two of Robespierre's friends, Louis de Saint-Just and Georges Couthon, were elected in their place. A week later, Robespierre was also placed on the committee. Danton left Paris to stay at his country home. With Marat dead and Danton gone, Robespierre was now the absolute leader of the Jacobins, and the most powerful man in France.

Victory in War and a Serious Step for the Government

Robespierre was in charge of a dreadful situation. France was on the verge of collapse. A British army was beseiging the port of Dunkirk, a British-Spanish fleet was menacing the port of Toulon, and uprisings against the revolution were now widespread.

However, in August, an army officer named Lazare Carnot was elected to the Committee of Public Safety. Carnot turned out to be a military genius. At Carnot's urging, on August 23, Robespierre and the committee decreed that everyone in France was now part of the army. Unmarried men were to be soldiers, married men were to work at making weapons and ammunition, women were to sew uniforms and tents for the troops, and even children were to make bandages for the wounded.

This made it seem to most people as if they were all doing great and important work for their country and for the revolution. French armies became filled with enthusiastic young recruits who were wildly patriotic. Because they believed they were making war to defend their people's freedom, these men were willing to risk their lives in fierce attacks that enemy troops, who were fighting only for pay, could not stand up to. French generals had also invented a new way of warfare that helped even more. Instead of fighting in long lines, French battalions were formed into huge, dense rectangles that could smash into a Prussian or Austrian line and shatter it. Throughout September and October, French armies won resounding victories. The British were pushed back from Dunkirk, the Austrians and Prussians were pushed out of France, and the port of Toulon was regained. The rebellions in the Vendée and in Lyons were put to an end in brutal fashion, with thousands of people executed by firing squads, the guillotine, and even by drowning.

As French armies were beginning to win against the foreign enemies, it seemed to Robespierre and the Jacobins that all-out war also had to be waged against the enemies of the revolution in France. They felt that law and order could be restored within France only by a program of terror and violence aimed at people who did not make the revolution the foremost thing in their lives.

The revolution was Robespierre's whole life. Nothing else mattered to him. He believed that the revolution could turn France into a perfect nation, and he wanted to do everything in his power, whatever it might take, to help that happen. Thus, he was perfectly willing to have thousands of people die if that would help the revolution.

So, in late summer of 1793, what was known as the Terror, or the Reign (rule) of Terror, began.

Chapter 10

The Terror and the Downfall of Robespierre

On September 3, 1793, the convention passed what was known as the Law of Suspected Persons. Anyone suspected of being against the revolution, or even of simply not working hard enough for the revolution, could be accused, arrested, and brought to trial by the Revolutionary Tribunal. If found guilty, the sentence was always death by guillotine.

One of the first sentenced by the law was the former queen, Marie Antoinette. She was accused of wasting enormous amounts of money, of persuading Louis to veto things, and of generally being an immoral person. None of these charges really deserved a death sentence, but they were regarded as proof that Marie Antoinette was against the revolution. She was sentenced to die. On October 14, she rode in the tumbrel with a number of others who had

An artist depicted Marie Antoinette just after being sentenced to death by the Revolutionary Tribunal.

Source Document

It is now sixteen or seventeen years since I saw the queen of France, then the dauphiness, at Versailles; and surely never lighted on the orb, which she hardly seemed to touch, a more delightful vision. I saw her just above the horizon, decorating and cheering the elevated sphere she had just begun to move in, glittering like the morning star full of life and splendor and joy. O, what a revolution! and what a heart must I have, to contemplate without emotion that elevation and that fall! . . . little did I dream that I should have lived to see such disasters fallen upon her, in a nation of gallant men, in a nation of men of honor, and of cavaliers! I thought ten thousand swords must have leaped from their scabbards, to avenge even a look that threatened her with insult.[1]

English political writer Edmund Burke wrote this description of his feelings about the death of French Queen Marie Antoinette.

been sentenced to be executed on the same day. She appeared calm, and many people thought she seemed proud. When the executioner lifted her severed head, the watching crowd broke into a roar of "Long live the republic!"

Soon after the former queen met her death, Brissot and twenty leading Girondins were put on trial. They were accused of seeking wealth and personal power. They were all condemned to death. On October 31, they all went to the guillotine together. Even one who managed to commit suicide first was beheaded anyway. Eight days later, Madame Roland was also executed. Her husband had escaped, but when he learned of her death, he committed suicide.

As time went on, no one was safe. Men who had been Third-Estate members of the National Assembly were guillotined. Generals who lost battles were guillotined. An elderly woman who had been a friend of King Louis's grandfather was guillotined. Even a number of sans-culottes and other common working people were guillotined.

The Terror was believed to be a way of keeping the revolution safe. But many Jacobins and most of the sans-culottes felt something else was needed. They believed that the Catholic religion had been nothing more than a way of keeping the peasants resigned to the rule of the king and the power of the nobles. Therefore, they decided that, to keep the revolution safe, it would be necessary to actually wipe out Christianity in France.

They began by totally changing the calendar. They did away with the seven-day week, replacing it with a ten-day period that had no Sunday. The months were also rearranged and given new names.

The Rise and Fall of the Hébertists

The Enraged Ones now had a leader by the name of Jacques-René Hébert, who was one of the most wildly fanatic of all French revolutionaries. Hébert wanted the Terror to be increased, wanted the prices of food and other goods controlled by the government, wanted all property divided up and distributed evenly among the people. He was also one of those who wanted to eliminate Christianity in France. He led his followers in destructive attacks on some of the Catholic cathedrals of Paris, breaking things and holding mock religious ceremonies at the altars. There were similar attacks throughout France, with many churches ransacked and partially destroyed, and used for wild ceremonies that mocked Catholic rituals. Priests were forced to renounce their beliefs, forced to stop holding services, and even forced to get married.

Robespierre was not a Catholic and not really even a Christian. Still, he did not approve of this attempt to destroy Christianity. He spoke against it in the convention, arguing that it made France look bad to the other countries of Europe.

Danton returned to Paris in November and took his place at the convention. He began to speak out against the Terror. "Perhaps the Terror once served a

Source Document

If the spring of popular government in time of peace is virtue, the springs of popular government in revolution are at once virtue and terror: virtue, without which terror is fatal; terror, without which virtue is powerless. Terror is nothing other than justice, prompt, severe, inflexible; it is therefore an emanation of virtue; it is not so much a special principle as it is a consequence of the general principle of democracy applied to our country's most urgent needs.[2]

Robespierre, criticized by many of his fellow citizens for his excessive use of execution to eliminate enemies, spoke out about the need for the use of terror.

useful purpose, but it should not hurt innocent people," he declared in one speech.[3] He also spoke against Hébert and his followers. Danton's friend, Camille Desmoulins, began to write articles in his newspaper, *The Old Cordelier*, condemning Hébert for being too extreme. Gradually, most of the members of the convention began to turn against the Hébertists.

On March 14, 1794, Hébert and the other Hébertist leaders were arrested and imprisoned. They were charged with planning to massacre the members of the convention and Jacobin Club in order to seize power and create a new government headed by Hébert and two others. It was also charged that they were being paid to do these things by agents of foreign governments. They were found guilty, and on Sunday, March 23, were all executed. Hébert was led to the guillotine, screaming in terror while the crowd laughed.

Now, Robespierre and Danton were the only two main leaders of the revolution left. Danton was immensely popular, but he did not have a clean record. There is considerable evidence that he probably took bribes during his time in government, even from the king.[4] To a person such as Robespierre, who was truly incorruptible, this would probably have made Danton seem like a traitor.

The Fall of Danton

Some historians believe that Robespierre deliberately set out to destroy Danton. Others think he just reluctantly went along with his supporters. He made two speeches in which he seemed to be defending Danton, stating that Danton had always appeared to be a vigorous fighter for the revolution. Nevertheless, on the night of March 30, Robespierre and all but two members of the Committee of Public Safety signed a warrant for the arrest of Danton and his supporters, including Camille Desmoulins. They were charged with being secretly in favor of a monarchy and being guilty of corruption—taking bribes and making money by means of their position in government.

On April 2, they went to trial at the convention. Danton defended himself in wild, fiery speeches, but he knew that the convention would not dare go against Robespierre. He was right. Robespierre made a speech in which he argued that, even though Danton had been a great patriot, he should not be spared.[5] He reminded the convention that Brissot and Hébert had been great patriots, too, but had not been spared. The convention listened to him, then voted that Danton and the others were guilty and sentenced them to be executed.

The execution was set for April 5. As the tumbrel carrying Danton, Desmoulins, and others creaked past the Duplay house where Robespierre lived, Danton yelled out, "You will follow us, Robespierre!"[6]

Danton was the last of the group to be executed. When he stepped onto the platform, it was soaked with the blood of the others. In a loud voice that could be heard by everyone in the first few rows around the platform, Danton said to the executioner, "Don't forget to show my head to the people. It is well worth the trouble."[7]

Just as he had not gone to see the king's execution, neither did Robespierre go to see any of these other executions.

Robespierre was now the undisputed head of the government of the French Republic. He immediately began to work at trying to create a perfect republic. For him, this meant a republic in which all people were truly equal, and all were moral and virtuous—that is,

As he was driven to his execution, Georges Danton (seen here) warned Robespierre that he, too, would face death at the hands of his fellow revolutionaries.

law-abiding, decent, and without sin. He felt that only religion could make people moral and virtuous, and so he decided the republic needed religion. However, he did not want to try to depend on any form of Christianity, so he literally created a new religion, in which the god was known simply as the Supreme Being. This was a sort of mixture of Christianity, some of the ideas of the Enlightenment, and the spirit of the revolution.

The Fall of Robespierre

On Sunday, June 8, Robespierre conducted a great celebration in honor of the Supreme Being. It was held in the same park where, a few years earlier, Lafayette's soldiers had fired into crowds of people. A miniature artificial mountain made of wood and plaster had been erected, at the top of which was an imposing statue. Dressed in a bright blue coat and wearing a crown of feathers on his head, Robespierre made a speech declaring that France was now showing the world that it believed in a Supreme Being and in immortality. There was an enormous crowd and there were hundreds of girls everywhere, throwing flowers. An orchestra played, people sang, and a number of cannons were fired in a salute. Robespierre appeared to be extremely happy, and most of the crowd enjoyed the spectacle. But many of the members of the convention, who had been ordered to be present, regarded all this as an example of Robespierre's growing desire to be in control of everything. Even

Source Document

Frenchmen, you war against kings; you are therefore worthy to honor Divinity. Being of Beings, Author of Nature, the brutalized slave, the vile instrument of despotism, the perfidious and cruel aristocrat, outrages Thee by his very invocation of Thy name. But the defenders of liberty can give themselves up to Thee, and rest with confidence upon Thy paternal bosom. Being of Beings, we need not offer to Thee unjust prayers. Thou knowest Thy creatures, proceeding from Thy hands. Their needs do not escape Thy notice, more than their secret thoughts. Hatred of bad faith and tyranny burns in our hearts, with love of justice and fatherland. Our blood flows for the cause of humanity. Behold our prayer. Behold our sacrifices. Behold the worship we offer Thee.[8]

When he took power during the revolution, Robespierre introduced some unusual changes. Among them was a devotion of the French nation to a "Supreme Being."

many of the sans-culottes were upset. Some of them grumbled that Robespierre was trying to become a new sort of pope!

Robespierre began to lose his popularity. Many members of the convention believed he was trying to become dictator (single ruler) of France. Resistance against him and his methods began to grow, secretly.

On July 26, Robespierre made a speech defending himself before the convention. He began in a low voice that gradually rose to a shout as he went on. He let the convention know that he was aware a plot was being hatched against him. He hinted that he knew who the plotters were, and that they would be rooted out and executed.

That night, Robespierre's opponents met together and decided that they must defend themselves. The next morning at the convention, one after another, they stood up and made speeches condemning Robespierre as a would-be dictator and bloodthirsty tyrant. When Robespierre tried to speak, he was drowned out by shouts of "A bas le tyrant" (Down with the tyrant)![9] Robespierre either became enraged, astounded, or terrified. Whatever the cause, he simply could not speak. He could only make choking noises in his throat. Someone yelled out, sarcastically, "The blood of Danton chokes him."[10] Robespierre staggered to a chair and sat down, putting his head in his hands. He listened silently as the convention voted to have him and his followers arrested.

The Execution of Robespierre

They were taken to the city hall and confined in the room where the Committee of Public Safety worked. But everything was confused now, and the people of Paris began taking sides. The members of the Commune and the Jacobin Club declared that the convention had committed treason, and called for revolt.

Other Parisians rushed to the convention hall, announcing their support for the convention.

Robespierre and his followers argued over what they should do, but could not come up with a good plan. Meanwhile, a horde of six thousand people, including many soldiers, headed for the city hall to seize the Robespierrists.

They broke into the building. Robespierre's brother, Augustin, who had come to Paris some months earlier, tried to escape through a window but fell to the street below and lay there badly injured. Louis de Saint-Just sat silent and motionless and let himself be captured. Couthon rushed to try to escape but fell down the stairs and suffered a head injury that knocked him unconscious.

No one knows exactly what happened to Maximilien Robespierre. One account says that he tried to shoot himself in the head, but only blew off part of his lower jaw. Another account says that a soldier shot him in the face. In either event, he remained alive with a shattered jaw, in terrible pain.

Robespierre was carried on a wooden board to a nearby room and put on a table. He lay there, semi-conscious, for a long time. Eventually, a doctor arrived and bandaged his mangled jaw.

At five o'clock on the afternoon of July 28, 1794, Robespierre and twenty-two of his followers were taken in carts to the guillotine. The crowd there was the largest that had ever watched any execution.

Maximilien Robespierre lies injured on the table in this artist's depiction of his arrest.

One by one, Robespierre's followers went under the blade.

Robespierre's eyes were closed, and he did not open them until he was carried up to the guillotine. He was placed in position. Either out of cruelty or because he felt it might interfere with the guillotine blade, the executioner bent over and tore the bandage from Robespierre's jaw. This must have been very painful, and Robespierre gave an agonized shriek.

It was the last sound he ever made.

Legacy of the Revolution

In the more than two hundred years since the French Revolution, historians have had many opinions about Maximilien Robespierre. Some have regarded him as a bloodthirsty monster, a dictator who was willing to kill thousands to have his way. Others have seen him as a sincere, dedicated man of the people, who believed in doing whatever he felt had to be done to give his country a government that was truly in the hands of the common people. But to this day, while there are statues of many other leaders of the revolution in places of honor in Paris, there is no statue of Robespierre. The people of France and the world still do not know what to make of Maximilien Robespierre. However, almost everyone agrees that Robespierre

Maximilien Robespierre, leader of the French Revolution, is remembered both for his firm commitment to democratic ideals and for the terror he used in trying to bring about change.

was probably the most important person who took part in the revolution—the one who had the greatest impact on the things that happened.

Following Robespierre's death, the Terror came to an end. The convention continued to govern, but slowly its power seeped away. There were several attempts by former nobles to seize control and turn France into a kingdom again, but they failed. However, there was a growing feeling against the power that working people had, and gradually the sans-culottes, the Jacobins, and other groups faded away.

On November 9, 1799, the popular and successful General Napoleon Bonaparte seized control of the government. He made himself dictator of France. With that, the revolution was over.

In the seventy-seven years following Robespierre's death, France had many kinds of government—once a dictatorship, twice a kingdom again, once more a republic, and two times an empire. In 1870, it became a republic again, and has remained one. But whatever the kind of government, the basic changes the revolution brought about were never lost. There were never again any restrictions based on class. The son of an ordinary farmer could become commander of the French Army, a cardinal of the Catholic Church, or the highest official of the government. Anyone willing to work hard could become wealthy and respected. Anyone could own property. There was freedom of religion, and generally, freedom of the press.

*Napoleon Bonaparte, the dictator who ended the French
Revolution by taking power in France, is seen here in a painting by
Antoine-Jean Gros.*

The French Revolution's effect has lasted to this day. French armies brought revolutionary ideas into other European countries. Some of those countries eventually had revolutions of their own. Nations that had long been ruled by nobles became republics and democracies, ruled by all the people.

The ideas of Robespierre, Danton, and others inspired new political ideas. Before the revolution, no country had any kind of government program for helping poor people. Robespierre and the Jacobins believed it was a government's duty to help. Today, many nations have government aid for the poor, and pensions and medical help for elderly people, which have their roots in the French Revolution.

Some of the ideas of the French Revolution inspired the twentieth-century political system called communism. This is a system based on the idea that all people should be absolutely equal in every way. The Russian Revolution of 1917 was much like the French Revolution. It gave Russia a form of communism for some seventy-five years. Today, the People's Republic of China regards itself as a Communist nation.

Many people see the French Revolution as a terrible event because of its violence and bloodshed. But like the American Revolution, it showed that common people could rise up and fight to gain freedom. The main idea of the French and American revolutions—that a nation's government should be in the hands of all its people—became widespread. These ideas are the basis for most governments in the world today.

Timeline

1789—*May 5*: The Estates-General meets in Versailles.

June 7: The Third Estate votes to name itself National Assembly.

June 20: The National Assembly delegates take the Tennis Court Oath.

June 23: The king orders the three estates to leave the meeting hall; The National Assembly refuses.

July 14: The Bastille is captured by a Paris mob.

Late July–Early August: Peasant revolts take place throughout France.

August 4: Feudalism ends in France.

August 26: The National Assembly produces the Declaration of the Rights of Man and the Citizen.

October 5: Six thousand women of Paris march to Versailles to demand bread.

October 6: The king and royal family are taken to Paris.

1790—*June 19*: Nobility is abolished.

July 12: The National Assembly decrees the Civil Constitution of the Clergy.

1791—*June 21*: The king and royal family attempt to escape from the country.

September 14: Louis accepts the constitution; France becomes a constitutional monarchy.

October 1: The Legislative Assembly meets as the new government of France.

1792—*April 20*: Declaration of war against Austria.

June 10: The king dismisses the Girondin ministers.

June 20: The Parisian sans-culottes invade the Tuileries.

Late July: The Prussian commander issues a threat against the city of Paris.

August 10: The sans-culottes invade the Tuileries and force the king to flee to the assembly for safety; The king is deposed.

August 13: The royal family is imprisoned in the Temple Prison.

September 2: The fortress of Verdun is captured by the Prussians; Prison massacres take place in Paris.

September 20: A French army defeats the Prussians.

September 21: The National Convention holds its first meeting.

September 21–22: The monarchy is abolished; France becomes a republic.

December: The trial of the king begins.

1793—*January 17*: The king is condemned to death.

January 21: The king is executed.

February 1: War is declared against Great Britain and the Dutch Republic.

March: Civil war begins in the Vendée; The Revolutionary Tribunal is created.

April 6: The Committee of Public Safety is created.

June 2: The Girondins are expelled from the convention and placed under house arrest.

July 27: Robespierre is appointed to the Committee of Public Safety; The Terror begins.

October 31: The Girondin leaders are executed.

1794—*March 14*: The Hébertist leaders are arrested.

March 23: The Hébertist leaders are executed.

March 30: Danton, Desmoulins, and other Dantonists are arrested.

April 5: The Dantonists are executed.

June 8: The Festival of the Supreme Being is held in Paris.

July 27: Robespierre and his supporters are arrested.

July 28: Robespierre and his supporters are executed; The Terror ends.

1799—Napoleon Bonaparte takes control of the government, making himself the dictator of France.

Chapter Notes

Chapter 2. A Troubled Nation

1. Arthur Young, "Travels During the Years 1787, 1788, and 1789," *North Park University History Department*, 1998, <http://www.campus/northpark.edu/history/Classes/ Sources/Young.html> (October 18, 1999).

2. Simon Schama, *Citizens: A Chronicle of the French Revolution* (New York: Alfred A. Knopf, 1989), p. 328.

Chapter 3. Rumblings of Revolt

1. Hanover College Department of History, "Cahier of 1789, The Third Estate of Versailles," *Hanover Historical Texts Project*, 1997, <http://history.hanover.edu/texts/ cahiers3.html> (October 18, 1999).

Chapter 4. A Day of Rage and Blood

1. Simon Schama, *Citizens: A Chronicle of the French Revolution* (New York: Alfred A. Knopf, 1989), p. 363.

2. J. M. Thompson, *The French Revolution* (Oxford, England: Basil Blackwell, 1964), p. 24.

3. Olivier Bernier, *Words of Fire, Deeds of Blood: The Mob, the Monarchy, and the French Revolution* (Boston: Little, Brown and Company, 1989), p. 17.

4. Jules Michelet, *History of the French Revolution* (Chicago: University of Chicago Press, 1967), p. 150.

5. Schama, p. 382.

6. Ibid.

Chapter 5. Great Changes and a Captive King

1. William C. Fray and Lisa A. Spar, "Declaration of the Rights of Man—1789," *The Avalon Project*, 1996, <http://www.yale.edu/lawweb/avalon/rightsof.htm> (October 18, 1999).

2. Simon Schama, *Citizens: A Chronicle of the French Revolution* (New York: Alfred A. Knopf, 1989), p. 467.

3. Christopher Hibbert, *The Days of the French Revolution* (New York: William Morrow and Company, Inc., 1980), p. 101.

4. M. J. Sydenham, *The French Revolution* (New York: G. P. Putnam's Sons, 1965), p. 61.

5. Olivier Bernier, *Words of Fire, Deeds of Blood: The Mob, the Monarchy, and the French Revolution* (Boston: Little, Brown and Company, 1989), p. 72.

6. Ibid., p. 73.

Chapter 6. Political Clubs, Disagreements, and an Escape Attempt

1. Hanover College Department of History, "The National Convention," *Hanover Historical Texts Project*, n.d., <http://history.hanover.edu/TEXTS/natcon.HTM> (October 18, 1999).

2. Simon Schama, *Citizens: A Chronicle of the French Revolution* (New York: Alfred A. Knopf, 1989), p. 554.

3. Olivier Bernier, *Words of Fire, Deeds of Blood: The Mob, the Monarchy, and the French Revolution* (Boston: Little Brown and Company, 1989), p. 279.

4. Frank Dwyer, *Danton* (New York: Chelsea House Publishers, 1987), p. 61.

Chapter 7. A War and the Downfall of a King

1. Simon Schama, *Citizens: A Chronicle of the French Revolution* (New York: Alfred A. Knopf, 1989), p. 580.

2. J. M. Thompson, *The French Revolution* (Oxford, England: Basil Blackwell, 1964), p. 256.

3. David P. Jordan, *The Revolutionary Career of Maximilien Robespierre* (New York: The Free Press, 1985), p. 86.

4. Christopher Hibbert, *The Days of the French Revolution* (New York: William Morrow and Company, Inc., 1980), p. 101.

5. Olivier Bernier, *Words of Fire, Deeds of Blood: The Mob, the Monarchy, and the French Revolution* (Boston: Little, Brown and Company, 1989), p. 6.

Chapter 8. The Birth of a Republic, the Death of a King

1. Christopher Hibbert, *The Days of the French Revolution* (New York: William Morrow and Company, Inc., 1980), p. 177.

2. Olivier Bernier, *Words of Fire, Deeds of Blood: The Mob, the Monarchy, and the French Revolution* (Boston: Little, Brown and Company, 1989), p. 391.

3. Hibbert, p. 184.

4. Simon Schama, *Citizens: A Chronicle of the French Revolution* (New York: Alfred A. Knopf, 1989), p. 665.

5. Ibid., p. 669.

6. Hibbert, p. 211.

Chapter 9. Civil War, a Trial, and a Murder

1. David L. Dowd, *The French Revolution* (New York: American Heritage, 1965), p. 118.

Chapter 10. The Terror and the Downfall of Robespierre

1. Paul Halsall, "Edmund Burke: The Death of Marie Antoinette," *Modern History Sourcebook*, August 1997, <http://www.fordham.edu/halsall/mod/1793burke.html> (October 18, 1999).

2. Paul Halsall, "Maximilien Robespierre: Justification of the Use of Terror," *Modern History Sourcebook,* August 1997, <http://www.fordham.edu/halsall/mod/robespierre-terror.html> (October 18, 1999).

3. Susan Banfield, *The Rights of Man, the Reign of Terror: The Story of the French Revolution* (New York: J. B. Lippincott, 1989), p. 162.

4. David P. Jordan, *The Revolutionary Career of Maximilien Robespierre* (New York: The Free Press, 1985), p. 247.

5. Christopher Hibbert, *The Days of the French Revolution* (New York: William Morrow and Company, Inc., 1980), p. 239.

6. Ibid., p. 248.

7. Simon Schama, *Citizens: A Chronicle of the French Revolution* (New York: Alfred A. Knopf, 1989), p. 820.

8. Paul Halsall, "Maximilien Robespierre: The Cult of the Supreme Being," *Modern History Sourcebook*, August 1997, <http://www.fordham.edu/halsall/mod/robespierre-supreme.html> (October 18, 1999).

9. J. M. Thompson, *The French Revolution* (Oxford, England: Basil Blackwell, 1964), p. 514.

10. Schama, p. 844.

Further Reading

Books

Banfield, Susan. *The Rights of Man, the Reign of Terror: The Story of the French Revolution*. New York: J. B. Lippincott, 1989.

Corzine, Phyllis. *The French Revolution*. San Diego, Calif.: Lucent Books, 1995.

Dwyer, Frank. *Danton*. New York: Chelsea House Publishers, 1987.

Otfinoski, Steven. *Triumph and Terror: The French Revolution*. New York: Facts on File, 1993.

Stewart, Gail B. *Life During the French Revolution*. San Diego, Calif.: Lucent Books, 1995.

Internet Addresses

Fray, William C., and Lisa A. Spar. *The Avalon Project.* 1996. <http://www.yale.edu/lawweb/avalon/rightsof.htm> (October 18, 1999).

Halsall, Paul. *Modern History Sourcebook*. August 1997. <http://www.fordham.edu/halsall/mod/1793burke.html> (October 18, 1999).

Hanover College Department of History. *Hanover Historical Texts Project.* 1997. <http://history.hanover.edu/texts/cahiers3.html> (October 18, 1999).

Index